The Athelings
Or
The Three Gifts
Vol. 3

by

Margaret Oliphant

The Athelings
Or
The Three Gifts
Vol. 3
by Margaret Oliphant

Copyright © 2023

All Rights reserved.

ISBN: 978-93-59956-44-2

Published by

DOUBLE 9 BOOKS

2/13-B, Ansari Road
Daryaganj, New Delhi – 110002
info@double9books.com
www.double9books.com
Tel. 011-40042856

This book is under public domain

ABOUT THE AUTHOR

Margaret Oliphant Wilson Oliphant was a Scottish author and historical writer who usually wrote under the name Mrs. Oliphant. She was born Margaret Oliphant Wilson on April 4, 1828, and died on June 20, 1897. She writes "domestic realism, the historical novel, and tales of the supernatural" as her short stories. Margaret Oliphant was born in Wallyford, near Musselburgh, East Lothian. She was the only daughter and youngest child still living of Margaret Oliphant (c. 1789-17 September 1854) and Francis W. Wilson, a clerk. We lived in Lasswade, Glasgow, and Liverpool when she was a child. In Wallyford, a street called Oliphant Gardens is named after her. As a girl, she was always trying new things with writing. Passages in the Life of Mrs. Margaret Maitland, her first book, came out in 1849. This was about the mostly successful Scottish Free Church movement, which was something her folks agreed with. Next came Caleb Field in 1851, the same year she met publisher William Blackwood in Edinburgh and was asked to write for Blackwood's Magazine. She did so for the rest of her life and wrote over 100 articles, including one that criticized Arthur Dimmesdale in Nathaniel Hawthorne's "The Scarlet Letter."

CONTENTS

BOOK III

CHAPTER I
AN OLD STORY

"Now, mother," said Charlie, "I'm in real earnest. My father would tell me himself if he were here. I want to understand the whole concern."

Mrs Atheling and her son were in Charlie's little room, with its one small lattice-window, overshadowed and embowered in leaves—its plain uncurtained bed, its small table, and solitary chair. Upon this chair, with a palpitating heart, sat Mrs Atheling, and before her stood the resolute boy.

And she began immediately, yet with visible faltering and hesitation, to tell him the story she had told the girls of the early connection between the present Lord Winterbourne and the Atheling family. But Charlie's mind was excited and preoccupied. He listened, almost with impatience, to the sad little romance of his father's young sister, of whom he had never heard before. It did not move him at all as it had moved Agnes and Marian. Broken hearts and disappointed loves were very far out of Charlie's way; something entirely different occupied his own imagination. He broke forth with a little effusion of impatience when the story came to an end. "And is this all? Do you mean to say this is the whole, mother? And my father had never anything to do with him but through a girl!"

"You are very unfeeling, Charlie," said Mrs Atheling, who wiped her eyes with real emotion, yet with a little policy too, and to gain time. "She was a dear innocent girl, and your father was very fond of her—reason enough to give him a dislike, if it were not sinful, to the very name of Lord Winterbourne."

"I had better go on with my packing, then," said Charlie. "So, that was all? I suppose any scamp in existence might do the same. Do you really mean to tell me, mother, that there was nothing but this?"

Mrs Atheling faltered still more under the steady observation of her son. "Charlie," said his mother, with agitation, "your father never would mention it to any one. I may be doing very wrong. If he only were here himself to decide! But if I tell you, you must give me your word never so much as to hint at it again."

Charlie did not give the necessary pledge, but Mrs Atheling made no pause. She did not even give him time to speak, however he might have been inclined, but hastened on in her own disclosure with agitation and excitement. "You have heard Papa tell of the young gentleman—he whom you all used to be so curious about—whom your father did a great benefit to," said Mrs Atheling, in a breathless hurried whisper. "Charlie, my dear, I never said it before to any creature—that was *him*."

She paused only a moment to take breath. "It was before we knew how he had behaved to dear little Bride," she continued, still in haste, and in an undertone. "What he did was a forgery—a forgery! people were hanged for it then. It was either a bill, or a cheque, or something, and Mr Reginald had written to it another man's name. It happened when Papa was in the bank, and before old Mr Lombard died—old Mr Lombard had a great kindness for your father, and we had great hopes then—and by good fortune the thing was brought to Papa. Your father was always very quick, Charlie—he found it out in a moment. So he told old Mr Lombard of it in a quiet way, and Mr Lombard consented he should take it back to Mr Reginald, and tell him it was found out, and hush all the business up. If your papa had not been so quick, Charlie, but had paid the money at once, as almost any one else would have done, it all must have been found out, and he would have been hanged, as certain as anything—he, a haughty young gentleman, and a lord's son!"

"And a very good thing, too," exclaimed Charlie; "saved him from doing any more mischief. So, I suppose now, it's all my father's blame."

"This Lord Winterbourne is a bad man," said Mrs Atheling, taking no notice of her son's interruption: "first he was furious to William, and then he cringed and fawned to him; and of course he had it on his conscience then about poor little Bride, though we did not know—and then he raved, and said he was desperate, and did not know what to do for money. Your father came home to me, quite unhappy about him; for he belonged to the same country, and everybody tried to make excuses for Mr Reginald, being a young man, and the heir. So William made it up in his own mind to go and tell the old lord, who was in London then. The old lord was a just man, but very proud. He did not take it kind of William, and he had no regard for Mr Reginald; but for the honour of the family he sent him away. Then we lost sight of him long, and Aunt Bridget took a dislike to us, and poor little Bride was dead, and we never heard anything of the Lodge or the Hall for many a year; but the old lord died abroad, and Mr Reginald came home Lord Winterbourne. That was all we ever knew. I thought your father had quite forgiven him, Charlie—we had other things to think of than keeping up old grudges—when all at once it came to be in the newspapers that Lord Winterbourne was a political man, that he was making speeches everywhere, and that he was to be one of the ministry. When your father saw that, he blazed up into such an anger! I said all I could, but William never minded me. He never was so bitter before, not even when we heard of little Bride. He said, Such a man to govern us and all the people!—a forger! a liar!—and sometimes, I think, he thought he would expose the whole story, and let everybody know."

"Time enough for that," said Charlie, who had listened to all this without comment, but with the closest attention. "What he did once he'll do again, mother; but we're close at his heels this time, and he won't get off now. I'm going to Oxford now to get some books. I say, mother, you'll be sure, upon your honour, not to tell the girls?"

"No, Charlie," said Mrs Atheling, with a somewhat faint affirmation; "but, my dear, I can't believe in it. It can't be true. Charlie, boy! if this was coming true, our Marian—your sister, Charlie!—why, Marian would be Lady Winterbourne!"

Charlie did not say a word in return; he only took down his little travelling-bag, laid it at his mother's feet to be packed, and left her to that business and her own meditations; but after he had left the room, the lad returned again and thrust in his shaggy head at the door. "Take care of Marian, mother," said Charlie, in a parting adjuration; "remember my father's little sister Bride."

So he went away, leaving Mrs Atheling a good deal disquieted. She had got over the first excitement of Miss Anastasia's great intelligence and the sudden preparations of Charlie. She had scarcely time enough, indeed, to give a thought to these things, when her son demanded this history from her, and sent her mind away into quite a different channel. Now she sat still in Charlie's room, pondering painfully, with the travelling-bag lying quite unheeded at her feet. At one moment she pronounced the whole matter perfectly impossible—at the next, triumphantly inconsequent, she leaped

to the full consummation of the hope, and saw her own pretty Marian—
dazzling vision!—the lady of Winterbourne! and again the heart of the
good mother fell, and she remembered little Bride. Louis, as he was now,
having no greater friends than their own simple family, and no pretensions
whatever either to birth or fortune, was a very different person from that
other Louis who might be heir of lands and lordship and the family pride
of the Riverses. Much perplexed, in great uncertainty and pain, mused
Mrs Atheling, half-resentful of that grand discovery of Miss Anastasia,
which might plunge them all into renewed trouble; while Charlie trudged
into Oxford for his Italian grammar—and Louis and Marian wandered
through the enchanted wood, drawing homeward—and Rachel sang to the
children—and Agnes wondered by herself over the secret which was to be
confided only to Mamma.

CHAPTER II
A CRISIS

That night Charlie had need of all his diplomatic talents. Before he returned from Oxford, his mother, by way of precaution lest Agnes should betray the sudden and mysterious visit of Miss Anastasia to Marian, contrived to let her elder daughter know mysteriously, something of the scope and object of the sudden journey for which it was necessary to prepare her brother, driving Agnes, as was to be supposed, into a very fever of suppressed excitement, joy, triumph, and anxiety. Mrs Atheling, conscious, hurried, and studying deeply not to betray herself—and Agnes, watching every one, stopping questions, and guarding off suspicions with prudence much too visible—were quite enough of themselves to rouse every other member of the little company to lively pursuit after the secret. Charlie was assailed by every shape and form of question: Where was he going—what was he to do? He showed no cleverness, we are bound to acknowledge, in evading these multitudinous interrogations; he turned an impenetrable front upon them, and made the most commonplace answers, making vast incursions all the time into Hannah's cakes and Mamma's bread-and-butter.

"He had to go back immediately to the office; he believed he had got a new client for old Foggo," said Charlie, with the utmost coolness; "making no secret of it at all," according to Mamma's indignant commentary.

"To the office!—are you only going home, after all?" cried Marian.

"I'll see when I get there," answered Charlie; "there's something to be done abroad. I shouldn't wonder if they sent *me*. I say, I wish you'd all come home at once, and make things comfortable. There's my poor father fighting it out with Susan. I should not stand it if it was me."

"Hold your peace, Charlie, and don't be rude," said Mrs Atheling. "But, indeed, I wish we were at home, and out of everybody's way."

"Who is everybody?" said Louis. "I, who am going myself, can wish quite sincerely that we were all at home; but the addition is mysterious— who is in anybody's way?"

"Mamma means to wish us all out of reach of the Evil Eye," said Agnes, a little romantically.

"No such thing, my dear. I daresay we could do *him* a great deal more harm than he can do us," said Mrs Atheling, with sudden importance and dignity; then she paused with a certain solemnity, so that everybody could perceive the grave self-restraint of the excellent mother, and that she could say a great deal more if she chose.

"But no one thinks what I am to do when you are all gone," said Rachel; and her tearful face happily diverted her companions from investigating and from concealing the secret. There remained among them all, however, a certain degree of excitement. Charlie was returning home to-morrow—specially called home on business!—perhaps to go abroad upon the same! The fact stirred all those young hearts with something not unlike envy. This boy seemed to have suddenly leaped in one day into a man.

And it was natural enough that, hearing of this, the mind of Louis should burn and chafe with fierce impatience. Charlie, who was perfectly undemonstrative of his thoughts and imaginations, was a very boy to Louis—yet there was need and occasion for Charlie in the crowd of life, when no one thought upon this fiery and eager young man. It was late that night when Louis left this only home and haven which he had ever known; and though he would fain have left Rachel there, his little sister would not remain behind him, but clung to his arm with a strange presentiment of something about to happen, which she could not explain. Louis scarcely answered a word to the quiet talk of Rachel as they went upon their way to the Hall. With difficulty, and even with impatience, he curbed his rapid stride to her timid little footsteps, and hurried her along without a glance at the surrounding scene, memorable and striking as it was. The broad moonlight flooded over the noble park of Winterbourne. The long white-columned front of the house—which was a great Grecian house, pallid, vast, and imposing—shone in the white light like a screen of marble; and on the great lawn immediately before it were several groups of people, dwarfed into minute miraculous figures by the great space and silence, and the intense illumination, which was far more striking and particular than the broader light of day. The chances were that Louis did not see them, as he plunged on, in the blindness of preoccupation, keeping no path, through light and shadow, through the trees and underwood, and across the broad unshaded greensward, where no one could fail to perceive him. His little sister clung to his arm in an agony of fear, grief, and confidence—trembling for something about to happen with an overpowering tremor—yet holding a vague faith in her brother, strange and absorbing. She said,

"Louis, Louis!" in her tone of appeal and entreaty. He did not hear her, but struck across the broad visible park, in the full stream of the moonlight, looking neither to the right hand nor to the left. As they approached, Rachel could not even hear any conversation among the groups on the lawn; and it was impossible to suppose that they had not been seen. Louis's abrupt direct course, over the turf and through the brushwood, must have attracted the notice of bystanders even in the daylight; it was still more remarkable now, when noiseless and rapid, through the intense white radiance and the perfect stillness, the stately figure of the young man, and his timid, graceful little sister, came directly forward in face of the spectators. These spectators were all silent, looking on with a certain fascination, and Rachel could not tell whether Louis was even conscious that any one was there.

But before they could turn aside into the road which led to the Hall door—a road to which Rachel most anxiously endeavoured to guide her brother—they were suddenly arrested by the voice of Lord Winterbourne. "I must put a stop to this," said his lordship suddenly and loudly, with so evident a reference to themselves, that even Rachel stopped without knowing it. "Here, young fellow, stop and give an account of yourself— what do you mean by wandering about my park at midnight, eh? I know your poaching practices. Setting snares, I suppose, and dragging about this girl as a protection. Get into your kennel, you mean dog; is this how you repay the shelter I have given you all your life?"

"It would be a fit return," said Louis. He did not speak so loud, but with a tremble of scorn and bitterness and intense youthful feeling in his voice, before which the echo of his persecutor's went out and died, like an ignoble thing. "If I were, as you say," repeated the young man, "setting snares for your game, or for your wealth, or for your life, you know it would be a fit return."

"Yes, I live a peaceful life with this villanous young incendiary under my roof!" said Lord Winterbourne. "I'll tell you what, you young ruffian, if nothing better can restrain you, locks and bars shall. Oh, no chance of appealing to *my* pity, with that fool of a girl upon your arm! You think you can defy me, year after year, because I have given charity to your base blood. My lad, you shall learn to know me better before another week is over our heads. Why, gentlemen, you perceive, by his own confession, I stand in danger of my life."

"Winterbourne," said some one over his shoulder, in a reproving tone, "*you* should be the last man in the world to taunt this unfortunate lad with his base blood."

Lord Winterbourne turned upon his heel with a laugh of insult which sent the wild blood dancing in an agony of shame, indignation, and rage even into Rachel's woman's face. "Well," said the voice of their tyrant, "I have supported the hound—what more would you have? His mother was a pretty fool, but she had her day. There's more of her conditions in the young villain than mine. I have no idea of playing the romantic father to such a son—not I!"

Louis did not know that he threw his sister off his arm before he sprang into the midst of these half-dozen gentlemen. She did not know herself, as she stood behind clenching her small fingers together painfully, with all the burning vehemence of a woman's passion. The young man sprang forward with the bound of a young tiger. His voice was hoarse with passion, not to be restrained. "It is a lie—a wilful, abominable lie!" cried Louis fiercely, confronting as close as a wrestler the ghastly face of his tyrant, who shrank before him. "I am no son of yours—you know I am no son of yours! I owe you the hateful bread I have been compelled to eat—nothing more. I am without a name—I may be of base blood—but I warn you for your life, if you dare repeat this last insult. It is a lie! I tell every one who condescends to call you friend; and I appeal to God, who knows that you know it is a lie! I may be the son of any other wretch under heaven, but I am not yours. I disown it with loathing and horror. Do you hear me?—you know the truth in your heart, and so do I!"

Lord Winterbourne fell back, step by step, before the young man, who pressed upon him close and rapid, with eyes which flamed and burned with a light which he could not bear. The insulting smile upon his bloodless face had not passed from it yet. His eyes, shifting, restless, and uneasy, expressed nothing. He was not a coward, and he was sufficiently quick-witted on ordinary occasions, but he had nothing whatever to answer to this vehement and unexpected accusation. He made an unintelligible appeal with his hand to his companions, and lifted up his face to the moonlight like a spectre, but he did not answer by a single word.

"Young man," said the gentleman who had spoken before, "I acknowledge your painful position, and that you have been addressed in a most unseemly manner—but no provocation should make you forget your natural duty. Lord Winterbourne must have had a motive for maintaining you as he has done. I put it to you calmly, dispassionately—what motive could he possibly have had, except one?"

"Ah!" said Louis, with a sudden and violent start, "he must have had a motive—it is true; he would not waste his cruel powers, even for cruelty's sake. If any man can tell me what child it was his interest to bastardise and defame, there may be hope and a name for me yet."

At these words, Lord Winterbourne advanced suddenly with a singular eagerness. "Let us have done with this foolery," he said, in a voice which was certainly less steady than usual; "I presume we can all be better employed than listening to the vapourings of this foolish boy. Go in, my lad, and learn a lesson by your folly to-night. I pass it over, simply because you have shown yourself to be a fool."

"I, however, do not pass it over, my lord," said Louis, who had calmed down after the most miraculous fashion, to the utter amazement of his sister. "Thank you for the provision you have given us, such as it is. Some time we may settle scores upon that subject. My sister and I must find another shelter to-night."

The bystanders were half disposed to smile at the young man's heroical withdrawal—but they were all somewhat amazed to find that Lord Winterbourne was as far as possible from sharing their amusement. He called out immediately in an access of passion to stop the young ruffian, incendiary, mischief-maker;—called loudly upon the servants, who began to appear at the open door—ordered Louis to his own apartment with the most unreasonable vehemence, and finally turned upon Rachel, calling her to give up the young villain's arm, and for her life to go home.

But Rachel was wound to the fever point as well as her brother. "No, no, it is all true he has said," cried Rachel. "I know it, like Louis; we are not your children—you dare not call us so now. I never believed you were our father—never all my life."

She exclaimed these words hastily in her low eager voice, as Louis drew her arm through his, and hurried her away. The young man struck again across the broad park and through the moonlight, while behind, Lord Winterbourne called to his servants to go after the fugitives—to bring that fellow back. The men only stared at their master, looked helplessly at each other, and went off on vain pretended searches, with no better intention than to keep out of Louis's way, until prudence came to the aid of Lord Winterbourne. "I shall scarcely think my life in safety while that young fool wanders wild about the country," he said to his friends, as he returned within doors; but his friends, one and all, thought this a very odd scene.

Meanwhile Louis made his rapid way with his little sister on his arm out over the glorious moonlit park of Winterbourne, away from the only home he had ever known—out to the night and to the world. Rachel, leaning closely upon him, scarcely so much as looked up, as her faltering footstep toiled to keep up with her brother. He, holding his proud young head high, neither turned nor glanced aside, but pressed on straight forward, as if to some visionary certain end before his eye. Then they came out at last to the white silent road, lying ghostlike under the excess of light—the quiet road which led through the village where all the houses slept and everything was still, not a curl of smoke in the moonlight, nor a house-dog's bark in the silence. It was midnight, vast and still, a great desolate uninhabited world. There was not a door open to them, nor a place where they could rest. But on pressed Louis, with the rapid step and unhesitating course of one who hastened to some definite conclusion. "Where are we going—where shall we go?" said poor little Rachel, drooping on his shoulder. Her brother did not hear her. He was not selfish, but he had not that superhuman consideration for others which might have broken the fiery inspiration of his own momentous thoughts, and made him think of the desolate midnight, and the houseless and outcast condition which were alone present to the mind of Rachel. He did not see a vast homeless solitude—a vagabond and disgraceful wandering, in this midnight walk. He saw a new world before him, such as had never glanced before across his fancy. "He must have had a motive," he muttered to himself. Rachel heard him sadly, and took the words as a matter of course. "Where are we to go?"—that was a more immediately important question to the simple mind of Rachel.

The Old Wood Lodge was as deep asleep as any house in the village. They paused, reluctant, both of them, to awake their friends within, and went back, pacing rapidly between the house of the Athelings and that of the Rector. The September night was cold, and Rachel was timid of that strange midnight world out of doors. They seemed to have nothing for it but pacing up and down upon the grassy road, where they were at least within sight of a friendly habitation, till morning came.

There was one light in one window of the Old Wood House; Rachel's eye went wandering to it wistfully, unawares: If the Rector knew—the Rector, who once would have been kind if Louis would have let him. But, as if in very response to her thoughts, the Rector, when they came back to this point again, was standing, like themselves, in the moonlight, looking over the low wall. He called to them rather authoritatively, asking what they did there—but started, and changed his tone into one of wondering interest and compassion when Rachel lifted her pale face to him, with the tears in her eyes. He hastened to the gate at once, and called them to enter. "Nay, nay, no hesitation—come in at once, that she may have rest and shelter," said the Rector in a peremptory tone, which, for the first time in his life, Louis had no thought of resenting. He went in without a word, leading his little sister. Perhaps it was the first great thing that ever had been done in all her life for Rachel's sake—for the sake of the delicate girl, who was half a child though a woman in years,—for sake of her tenderness, her delicate frame, her privilege of weakness. The two haughty young men went in silently together into this secluded house, which never opened its doors to any guest. It was an invalid's home, and some one was always at hand for its ailing mistress. By-and-by Rachel, in the exhaustion of great excitement, fell asleep in a little quiet room looking over that moonlit park of Winterbourne. Louis, who was in no mood for sleep, watched below, full of eager and unquiet thoughts. They had left Winterbourne Hall suddenly; the Rector asked no further questions, expressed no wonder, and left the young man who had repelled him once, with a lofty and dignified hospitality, to his meditations or repose.

CHAPTER III
CHARLIE'S PREPARATIONS

Charlie Atheling was not at all of an imaginative or fanciful turn of mind. His slumbers were not disturbed by castle-building—he wasted none of his available time in making fancy sketches of the people, or the circumstances, among which he was likely to be thrown. He was not without the power of comprehending at a glance the various features of his mission; but by much the most remarkable point of Charlie's character was his capacity for doing his immediate business, whatever that might be, with undivided attention, and with his full powers. On this early September morning he neither occupied himself with anticipations of his interview with Miss Anastasia, nor his hurried journey. He did not suffer his mind to stray to difficult questions of evidence, nor wander off into speculations concerning what he might have to do when he reached the real scene of his investigation. What he had to do at the moment he did like a man, bending upon his serious business all the faculties of his mind, and all the furrows of his brow. He got up at six o'clock, not because he particularly liked it, but because these early morning hours had become his habitual time for extra work of every kind, and sat upon Hannah's bench in the garden, close by the kitchen door, with the early sun and the early wind playing hide-and-seek among his elf-locks, learning his Italian grammar, as if this was the real business for which he came into the world.

"Whatsoever thy hand findeth to do"—that was Charlie's secret of success. He had only a grammar, a dictionary, and a little New Testament in Italian—and he had not at this moment the slightest ambition to read Dante in the original; but with steady energy he chased those unknown verbs into the deep caverns of his memory—a memory which was prodigious, and lost nothing committed to it. The three books accompanied him when he went in to breakfast, and marched off in his pocket to Oxford when it was time to keep his appointment with Miss Anastasia. Meanwhile the much-delayed travelling-bag only now began to get packed, and Mrs Atheling, silently toiling at this business, felt convinced that Susan would mislay all the things most important for Charlie's comfort, and very much yearned in her heart to accompany her son home. They were to meet him at the railway, whence he would depart immediately, after his interview with Miss Rivers; and Charlie's secret commission made a considerable deal of excitement in the quiet little house.

Miss Anastasia, who was much too eager and impetuous to be punctual, had been waiting for some time, when her young agent made his appearance at the office of her solicitor. After she had charged him with being too late, and herself suffered conviction as being too early, the old lady proceeded at once to business; they were in Mr Temple's own room, but they were alone.

"I have made copies of everything that seemed to throw light upon my late father's wanderings," said Miss Anastasia—"not much to speak of— see! These papers must have been carefully weeded before they came to my hands. Here is an old guide-book marked with notes, and here a letter dated from the place where he died. It is on the borders of Italy—at the foot of the Alps—on the way to Milan, and not very far from there. You will make all speed, young Atheling; I trust to your prudence—betray nothing—do not say a word about these children until you find some certain clue. It is more than twenty years—nearly one-and-twenty years—since my father died; but a rich Englishman, who married among them, was not like to be forgotten in such a village. Find out who this Giulietta was—if you can discover the family, they might know something. My father had an attendant, a sort of courier, who was with us often—Jean Monte, half a Frenchman half an Italian. I have never heard of him since that time; he might be heard of on the way, and *he* might know—but I cannot direct you, boy—I trust to your own spirit, your own foresight, your own prudence. Make haste, as if it was life and death; yet if time will avail you, take time. Now, young Atheling, I trust you!—bring clear evidence—legal evidence—what will stand in a court of law—and as sure as you live your fortune is made!"

Charlie did not make a single protestation in answer to this address. He folded up carefully those fragments of paper copied out in Miss Anastasia's careful old-fashioned lady's hand, and placed them in the big old pocket-book which he carried for lack of a better.

"I don't know much of the route," said Charlie,—"over the Alps, I suppose," and for once his cheek flushed with the youthful excitement of the travel. "I shall find out all about that immediately when I get to town;

and there is a passport to be seen after. When I am ready to start—which will be just as soon as the thing can be done—I shall let you know how I am to travel, and write immediately when I arrive there;—I know what you mean me to do."

Then Miss Anastasia gave him—(a very important part of the business)—two ten-pound notes, which was a very large sum to Charlie, and directed him to go to the banking-house with which she kept an account in London, and get from them a letter of credit on a banker in Milan, on whom he could draw, according to his occasions. "You are very young, young Atheling," said Miss Rivers; "many a father would hesitate to trust his son as I trust you; but I'm a woman and an optimist, and have my notions: you are only a boy, but I believe in you—forget how young you are while you are about my business—plenty of time after this for enjoying yourself—and I tell you again, if you do your duty, your fortune is made."

The old lady and the youth went out together, to where the little carriage and the grey ponies stood at the solicitor's door. Charlie, in his present development, was not at all the man to hand a lady with a grace to her carriage; nor was this stately gentlewoman, in her brown pelisse, at all the person to be so escorted; but they were a remarkable pair enough, as they stood upon the broad pavement of one of the noblest streets of Christendom. Miss Anastasia held out her hand with a parting command and warning, as she took her seat and the reins.—"Young Atheling, remember! it is life and death!"

She was less cautious at that moment than she had been during all their interview. The words full upon another ear than his to whom they were addressed. Lord Winterbourne was making his way at the moment with some newly-arrived guests of his, and under the conduct of a learned pundit from one of the colleges, along this same picturesque High Street; and, in the midst of exclamations of rapture and of interest, his suspicious and alarmed eye caught the familiar equipage and well-known figure of Miss Anastasia. Her face was turned in the opposite direction,—she did not see him,—but a single step brought him near enough to hear her words. "Young Atheling!" Lord Winterbourne had not forgotten his former connection with the name, but the remembrance had long lain dormant in a breast which was used to potent excitements. William Atheling, though he once saved a reckless young criminal, could do no harm with his remote unbelievable story to a peer of the realm,—a man who had sat in the councils of the State. Lord

Winterbourne had begun his suit for the Old Wood Lodge with the most contemptuous indifference to all that could be said of him by any one of this family; yet somehow it struck him strangely to hear so sudden a naming of this name. "Young Atheling!" He could not help looking at the youth,—meeting the stormy gleam in the eyes of Charlie, whose sudden enmity sprung up anew in an instant. Lord Winterbourne was sufficiently disturbed already by the departure of Louis, and with the quick observation of alarm remarked everything. He could understand no natural connection whatever between this lad and Miss Anastasia. His startled imagination suggested instantly that it bore some reference to Louis, and what interpretation was it possible to give to so strange an adjuration—"It is life and death!"

CHAPTER IV
GOING AWAY

"Charlie, my dear boy," said Mrs Atheling, with a slight tremble in her voice, "I suppose it may be months before we see you again."

"I can't tell, mother; but it will not be a day longer than I can help," said Charlie, who had the grace to be serious at the moment of parting. "There's only one thing, you know,—I must do my business before I come home."

"And take care of yourself," said Mrs Atheling; "take great care when you are going over those mountains, and among those people where bandits are—you know what stories we have read about such robbers, Charlie,—and remember, though I should be very glad to hear good news about Louis, Louis is not my own very boy, like you."

"Hush, mother—no need for naming him," said Charlie; "he is of more moment than me, however, this time—for that's my business. Never fear—thieves may be fools there as well as at home, but they're none such fools as to meddle with me. Now, mother, promise me, the last thing,—Agnes, do you hear?—don't tell Marian a word, nor *him*. I'll tell old Foggo the whole story, and Foggo will do what he can for him when he gets to London; but don't you go and delude him, telling him of this, for it would just be as good as ruin if I don't succeed; and it all may come to nothing, as like as not. I say, Agnes, do you hear?"

"Yes, I hear, very well; but I am not given to telling secrets," said Agnes, with a little dignity.

Charlie only laughed as he arranged himself in the corner of the second-class carriage, and drew forth his grammar; there was no time for anything more, save entreaties that he would write, and take care of himself; and the train flashed away, leaving them somewhat dull and blank in the reaction of past excitement, looking at each other, and half reluctant to turn their faces homeward. Their minds hurried forth, faster than either steam or electricity, to the end of Charlie's journey. They went back with very slow steps and very abstracted minds. What a new world of change and sudden revolution might open upon them at Charlie's return!

Mrs Atheling had some business in the town, and the mother and daughter pursued their way silently to that same noble High Street where Charlie had seen Lord Winterbourne, and where Lord Winterbourne and his party were still to be caught sight of, appearing and reappearing by glimpses as they "did" the halls and colleges. While her mother managed some needful business in a shop, Agnes stood rather dreamily looking down the stately street; its strange old-world mixture of the present and the past; its union of all kinds of buildings; the trim classic pillars and toy cupolas of the eighteenth century—the grim crumbling front of elder days—the gleams of green grass and waving trees through college gateways—the black-gowned figures interrupting the sunshine—the beautiful spire striking up into it as into its natural element,—a noble hyacinthine stem of immortal flowers. Agnes did not know much about artistic effect, nor anything about orders of architecture, but the scene seized upon her imagination, as was its natural right. Her thoughts were astray among hopes and chances far enough out of the common way—but any dream of romance could make itself real in an atmosphere like this.

She was pale,—she was somewhat of an abstracted and musing aspect. When one took into consideration her misfortune of authorship, she was in quite a sentimental *pose* and attitude—so thought her American acquaintance, who had managed to secure an invitation to the Hall, and was one of Lord Winterbourne's party. But Mr Endicott had "done" all the colleges before, and he could afford to let his attention be distracted by the appearance of the literary sister of the lady of his love.

"I am not surprised at your abstraction," said Mr Endicott. "In this, indeed, I do not hesitate to confess, my country is not equal to your Island. What an effect of sunshine! what a breadth of shade! I cannot profess to have any preference, in respect to Art, for the past, picturesque though it be—a poet of these days, Miss Atheling, has not to deal with facts, but feelings; but I have no doubt, before I interrupted you, the whole panorama of History glided before your meditative eye."

"No, indeed; I was thinking more of the future than of the past," said Agnes hurriedly.

"The future of this nation is obscure and mysterious," said Mr Endicott, gathering his eyebrows solemnly. "Some man must arise to lead you — to glory — or to perdition! I see nothing but chaos and darkness; but why should I prophesy? A past generation had leisure to watch the signs of the times; but for us 'Art is long and time is fleeting,' and happy is the man who can snatch one burning experience from the brilliant mirage of life."

Agnes, a little puzzled by this mixture of images, did not attempt any answer. Mr Endicott went on.

"I had begun to observe, with a great deal of interest, two remarkable young minds placed in a singular position. They were not to be met, of course, at the table of Lord Winterbourne," said the American with dignity; "but in my walks about the park I sometimes encountered them, and always endeavoured to draw them into conversation. So remarkable, in fact, did they seem to me, that they found a place in my Letters from England; studies of character entirely new to my consciousness. I believe, Miss Atheling, I had once the pleasure of seeing them in your company. They stand — um — unfortunately in a — a — an equivocal relationship to my noble host."

"Ah! what of them?" cried Agnes quickly, and with a crimsoned cheek. She felt already how difficult it was to hear them spoken of, and not proclaim at once her superior knowledge.

"A singular event, I understand, happened last night," continued Mr Endicott. "Viscount Winterbourne, on his own lawn, was attacked and insulted by the young man, who afterwards left the house under very remarkable circumstances. My noble friend, who is an admirable example of an old English nobleman, was at one time in actual danger, and I believe has been advised to put this fiery youth —"

"Do you mean Louis?" cried Agnes, interrupting him anxiously. "Louis! — do you mean that he has left the Hall?"

"I am greatly interested, I assure you, in tracing out this romance of real life," said Mr Endicott. "He left the Hall, I understand, last evening — and my noble friend is advised to take measures for his apprehension. I look upon the whole history with the utmost interest. How interesting to trace the motives of this young mind, perhaps the strife of passions — gratitude mixing with a sense of injury! If he is secured, I shall certainly visit him: I know no nobler subject for a drama of passion; and dramas of the passions are what we want to ennoble this modern time."

"Mother!" cried Agnes, "mother, come; we have no time to lose—Mr Endicott has told me—Mamma, leave these things to another time. Marian is alone; there is no one to support her. Oh, mother, mother! make haste! We must go home!"

She scarcely gave a glance to Mr Endicott as he stood somewhat surprised, making a study of the young author's excitable temperament for his next "letter from England"—but hastened her mother homeward, explaining, as she went, though not very coherently, that Louis had attacked Lord Winterbourne—that he had left the Hall—that he had done something for which he might be apprehended. The terror of disgrace—that most dread of all fears to people in their class—overwhelmed both mother and daughter, as they hastened, at a very unusual pace, along the road, terrified to meet himself in custody, or some one coming to tell them of his crime. And Marian, their poor beautiful flower, on whom this storm would fall so heavily—Marian was alone!

CHAPTER V
THE OLD WOOD HOUSE

Louis passed the night in the Rector's library. He had no inclination for sleep; indeed, he was almost scornful of the idea that he *could* sleep under his new and strange circumstances; and it was not until he roused himself, with a start, to see that the pale sheen of the moonlight had been succeeded by the rosy dawn of morning, that he knew of the sudden, deep slumber, that had fallen upon him. It was morning, but it was still a long time till day; except the birds among the trees there was nothing astir, not even the earliest labourer, and he could not hear a sound in the house. All the events of the previous night returned upon Louis's mind with all the revived freshness of a sudden awaking. A great change had passed upon him in a few hours. He started now at once out of the indefinite musings, the flush of vain ambition, the bitter brooding over wrong which had been familiar to his mind. He began to think with the earnest precision of a man who has attained to a purpose. Formerly it had been hard enough for his proud undisciplined spirit, prescient of something greater, to resolve upon a plan of tedious labour for daily bread, or to be content with such a fortune as had fallen to such a man as Mr Atheling. Even with love to bear him out, and his beautiful Marian to inspire him, it was hard, out of all the proud possibilities of youth, to plunge into such a lot as this. Now he considered it warily, with the full awakened consciousness of a man. Up to this time his bitter dislike and opposition to Lord Winterbourne had been carried on by fits and starts, as youths do contend with older people under whose sway they have been all their life. He took no reason with him when he decided that he was not the son of the man who opposed him. He never entered into the question how he came to the Hall, or what was the motive of its master. He had contented himself with a mere unreasoning conviction that Lord Winterbourne was not his father; but only one word was wanted to awaken the slumbering mind of the youth, and that word had been spoken last night. Now a clear and evident purpose became visible before him. What was Lord Winterbourne's reason for keeping him all his life under so killing a bondage? What child was there in the world whom it was Lord Winterbourne's interest to call illegitimate and keep in obscurity? His heart swelled—the colour rose in his face. He did not see how hopeless was the search—how entirely without grounds, without information, he was. He did not perceive how vain, to every reasonable individual, would seem the fabric he had built upon a mere conviction of his own. In his own eager perception everything was possible to that courage, and perseverance indomitable, which he felt to be in him; and, for the first time in his life, Louis came down from the unreasonable and bitter pride which had shut his heart against all overtures of friendship. Friendship—help—advice—the aid of those who knew the world better than he did—these were things to be sought for, and solicited now. He sat in the Rector's chair, leaning upon the Rector's writing-table; it was not without a struggle that he overcame his old repugnance, his former haughtiness. It was not without a pang that he remembered the obligation under which this stranger had laid him. It was his first effort in self-control, and it was not an easy one; he resolved at last to ask counsel from the Rector, and lay fully before him the strange circumstances in which he stood.

The Rector was a man of capricious hours, and uncertain likings. He was sometimes abroad as early as the earliest ploughman; to-day it was late in the forenoon before he made his appearance. Breakfast had been brought to Louis, by himself, in the library; in this house they were used to solitary meals at all hours—and he had already asked several times for the Rector, when Mr Rivers at last entered the room, and saluted him with stately courtesy. "My sister, I find, has detained your sister," said the Rector. "I hope you have not been anxious—they tell me the young lady will join us presently."

Then there was a pause; and then Mr Rivers began an extremely polite and edifying conversation, which must have reminded any spectator of the courtly amity of a couple of Don Quixotes preparing for the duello. The Rector himself conducted it with the most solemn gravity imaginable. This Lionel Rivers, dissatisfied and self-devouring, was not a true man. Supposing himself to be under a melancholy necessity of disbelieving on pain of conscience, he yet submitted to an innumerable amount of practical shams, with which his conscience took no concern. In spite of his great talents, and of a character full of natural nobleness, when you came to its foundations, a false tone, an artificial strain of conversation, an unreal and insincere expression, were unhappily familiar enough to the dissatisfied clergyman, who vainly tried to anchor himself upon the authority of the Church. Louis, on the contrary, knew nothing of talk which was a mere veil and concealment of meaning; he could not use vain words when his heart burned within him; he had no patience for those conversations which were merely intended to occupy time, and which meant and led to nothing. Yet it was very difficult for him, young, proud, and inexperienced as he was, without any invitation or assistance from his companion, to enter upon his explanation. He changed colour, he became uneasy, he scarcely answered the indifferent remarks addressed to him. At length, seeing nothing better for it, he plunged suddenly and without comment into his own tale.

"We have left Winterbourne Hall," said Louis, reddening to his temples as he spoke. "I have long been aware how unsuitable a home it was for me. I am going to London immediately. I cannot thank you enough for your hospitality to my sister, and to myself, last night."

"That is nothing," said the Rector, with a motion of his hand. "Some time since I had the pleasure of saying to your friends in the Lodge that it would gratify me to be able to serve you. I do not desire to pry into your plans; but if I can help you in town, let me know without hesitation."

"So far from prying," said Louis, eagerly, interrupting him, "I desire nothing more than to explain them. All my life," and once again the red blood rushed to the young man's face,—"all my life I have occupied the most humiliating of positions—you know it. I am not a meek man by nature; what excuse I have had if a bitter pride has sometimes taken possession of me, you know——"

The Rector bowed gravely, but did not speak. Louis continued in haste, and with growing agitation, "I am not the son of Lord Winterbourne—I am not a disgraced offshoot of your family—I can speak to you without feeling shame and abasement in the very sound of your name. This has been my conviction since ever I was capable of knowing anything—but Heaven knows how subtly the snare was woven—it seemed impossible, until now when we have done it, to disengage our feet."

"Have you made any discovery, then? What has happened?" said the Rector, roused into an eager curiosity. Here, at the very outset, lay Louis's difficulty—and he had never perceived it before.

"No; I have made no discovery," he said, with a momentary disconcertment. "I have only left the Hall—I have only told Lord Winterbourne what he knows well, and I have known long, that I am not his son."

"Exactly—but how did you discover that?" said the Rector.

"I have discovered nothing—but I am as sure of it as that I breathe," answered Louis.

The Rector looked at him—looked at a portrait which hung directly above Louis's head upon the wall, smiled, and shook his head. "It is quite natural," he said; "I can sympathise with any effort you make to gain a more honourable position, and to disown Lord Winterbourne—but it is vain, where there are pictures of the Riverses, to deny your connection with my family. George Rivers himself, my lord's heir, the future head of the family, has not a tithe as much of the looks and bearing of the blood as you."

Louis could not find a word to say in face of such an argument—he looked eagerly yet blankly into the face of the Rector—felt all his pulses throbbing with fiery impatience of the doubt thus cast upon him—yet knew nothing to advance against so subtle and unexpected a charge of kindred, and could only repeat, in a passionate undertone, "I am not Lord Winterbourne's son."

"I do not know," said the Rector, "I have no information which is not common to all the neighbourhood—yet I beg you to guard against delusion. Lord Winterbourne brought you here while you were an infant—since then you have remained at the Hall—he has owned you, I suppose, as much as a man ever owns an illegitimate child. Pardon me, I am obliged to use the common words. Lord Winterbourne is not a man of extended benevolence, neither is he one to take upon himself the responsibility or blame of another. If you are not his son, why did he bring you here?"

Louis raised his face from his hands which had covered it—he was very pale, haggard, almost ghastly. "If you can tell me of any youth—of any child—of any man's son, whom it was his interest to disgrace and remove out of the way," said the young man with his parched lips, "I will tell you why I am here."

The Rector could not quite restrain a start of emotion—not for what the youth said, for that was madness to the man of the world—but for the extreme passion, almost despair, in his face. He thought it best to soothe rather than to excite him.

"I know nothing more than all the world knows," said Mr Rivers; "but, though I warn you against delusions, I will not say you are wrong when you are so firmly persuaded that you are right. What do you mean to do in London—can I help you there?"

Louis felt with no small pang this giving up of the argument—as if it were useless to discuss anything so visionary—but he roused himself to answer the question: "The first thing I have to do," he said quickly, "is to maintain my sister and myself."

The Rector bowed again, very solemnly and gravely—perhaps not without a passing thought that the same duty imposed chains more galling than iron upon himself.

"That done, I will pursue my inquiries as I can," said Louis; "you think them vain—but time will prove that. I thank you now, for my sister's sake, for receiving us—and now we must go on our way."

"Not yet," said the Rector. "You are without means, of course—what, do you think it a disgrace, that you blush for it?—or would you have me suppose that you had taken money from Lord Winterbourne, while you deny that you are his son? For this once suppose me your friend; I will supply you with what you are certain to need; and you can repay me—oh, with double interest if you please!—only do not go to London unprovided— for that is the maddest method of anticipating a heartbreak; your sister is young, almost a child, tender and delicate—let it be, for her sake."

"Thank you; I will take it as you give it," said Louis. "I am not so ungenerous as you suppose."

There was a certain likeness between them, different as they were— there was a likeness in both to these family portraits on the walls. Before such silent witnesses Louis's passionate disclaimer, sincere though it was, was unbelievable. For no one could believe that he was not an offshoot of the house of Rivers, who looked from his face and the Rector's to those calm ancient faces on the walls.

CHAPTER VI
AN ADVENTURER

"They have left the Hall."

That was all Marian said when she came to the door to meet her mother and sister, who paused in the porch, overcome with fatigue, haste, and anxiety. Mrs Atheling was obliged to pause and sit down, not caring immediately to see the young culprit who was within.

"And what has happened, Marian,—what has happened? My poor child, did he tell you?" asked Mrs Atheling.

"Nothing has happened, mamma," said Marian, with a little petulant haste; "only Louis has quarrelled with Lord Winterbourne; but, indeed, I wish you would speak to him. Oh, Agnes, go and talk to Louis; he says he will go to London to-day."

"And so he should; there is not a moment to be lost," said Agnes,—"I will go and tell him; we can walk in with him to Oxford, and see him safely away. Tell Hannah to make haste, Marian,—he must not waste an hour."

"What does she mean,—what is the matter? Oh, what have you heard, mamma?" said Marian, growing very pale.

"Hush, dear; I daresay it was not him,—it was Mr Endicott, who is sure to hate him, poor boy; he said Lord Winterbourne would put him in prison, Marian. Oh," said Mrs Atheling, getting up hurriedly, "he ought to go at once to Papa."

But they found Louis, whom they all surrounded immediately with terror, sympathy, and encouragement, entirely unappalled by the threatened vengeance of Lord Winterbourne.

"There is nothing to charge me with; he can bring no accusation against me; if he did ever say it, it must have been a mere piece of bravado," said Louis; "but it is better I should go at once without losing an hour, as Agnes says. Will you let Rachel stay? and you, who are the kindest mother in the world, when will you have compassion on us and come home?"

"Indeed, I wish we were going now," said Mrs Atheling; and she said it with genuine feeling, and a sigh of anxiety. "You must tell Papa we will not stay very long; but I suppose we must see about this lawsuit first; and I am sure I cannot tell who is to manage it now, since Charlie is gone."

"Shall you go to Papa at once, Louis?" asked Marian, who was very anxious to conceal from every one the tears in her downcast eyes.

"Surely, at once," said Louis. "We are in different circumstances now; I have a great deal to ask any one who knows the family of Rivers. Do you know it never before occurred to me that Lord Winterbourne must have had some powerful inducement for keeping me here, knowing as well as I do that I am not his son."

Mrs Atheling and Agnes turned a sudden guilty look upon each other; but neither had betrayed the secret;—what did he mean?

"Unless it was his interest in some way—unless it was for his evident advantage to disgrace and disable me," said Louis, groping in the dark, when they knew one possible solution of the mystery so well, "I am convinced he never would have kept me as he has done at the Hall."

He spoke in a tone different to that which he had used to the Rector, and very naturally different—for Louis here was triumphant in the faith of his audience, and did not hesitate to say all he felt, nor fear too close an investigation into the grounds of his belief. He spoke fervently; and Marian and Rachel looked at him with the faith of enthusiasm, and Mrs Atheling and Agnes with wonder, agitation, and embarrassment. But, as he went on, it became too much for the self-control of the good mother. She hurried out on pretence of superintending Hannah, and was very soon followed by Agnes. "I durst not stay, I should have told him," said Mrs Atheling, in a hurried whisper. "Who could put so much into his head, Agnes? who could lead him so near the truth?—only God! My dear child, I believe in it all now."

Agnes had believed in it all from the first moment of hearing it, but so singular a strain was upon the minds of both mother and daughter, knowing this extraordinary secret which the others did not know, that it was not wonderful they should give a weight much beyond their desert to the queries of Louis. Yet, indeed, Louis's queries took a wonderfully correct direction, and came very near the truth.

It was a day of extreme agitation to them all, and not until Louis, who had no travelling-bag to pack, had been accompanied once more to the railway, and seen safely away, with many a lingering farewell, was any one able to listen to, or understand, Rachel's version of the events of last night. When he was quite gone—when it was no longer possible to wave a hand to him in the distance, or even to see the flying white plume of the miraculous horseman who bounded along with all that line of carriages, the three girls came home together through the quiet evening road—the disenchanted road, weary and unlovely, which Marian marvelled much any one could prefer to Bellevue. They walked very close together, with Marian in the midst, comforting her in an implied, sympathetic, girlish fashion—for Rachel, though Louis had belonged to her so very much longer, and was her sole authority, law-giver, and hero, instinctively kept her own feelings out of sight, and took care of Marian. These girls were very loyal to their own visionary ideas of the mysterious magician who had not come to either of them yet, but whose coming both anticipated some time, with awe and with smiles.

And then Rachel told them how it had fared with her on the previous night. Rachel had very little to say about the Rector; she had given him up conscientiously to Agnes, and with a distant and reverent admiration of his loftiness, contemplated him afar off, too great a person for her friendship. "But in the morning the maid came and took me to Miss Rivers—did you ever see Miss Rivers?—she is very pale—and pretty, though she is old, and a very, very great invalid," said Rachel. "Some one has to sit up with her every night, and she has so many troubles—headaches, and pains in her side, and coughs, and every sort of thing! She told me all about them as she lay on the sofa in her pretty white dressing-gown, and in *such* a soft voice as if she was quite used to them, and did not mind. Do you think you could be a nurse to any one who was ill, Agnes?"

"She *has* been a nurse to all of us when we were ill," said Marian, rousing herself for the effort, and immediately subsiding into the pensiveness which the sad little beauty would not suffer herself to break, even though she began in secret to be considerably interested about the interior of the mysterious Wood House, and the invisible Miss Rivers. Marian thought Louis would not be pleased if he could imagine her thinking of any one but him, so soon after he had gone away.

"But I don't mean at home—I mean a stranger," said Rachel, "one whom you did not *love*. I think it must be rather hard sometimes; but do you know I was very nearly offering to be nurse to Miss Rivers, she spoke so kindly to me? And then Louis will have to work," continued the faithful little sister, with tears in her eyes; "you must tell me what I can do, Agnes, not to be a burden upon Louis. Oh, do you think any one would give me money for singing now?"

CHAPTER VII
LORD WINTERBOURNE

Lord Winterbourne, all his life, had been a man of guile; he was so long experienced in it, that dissimulation became easy enough to him, when he was not startled or thrown suddenly off his guard. Already every one around him supposed he had quite forgiven and forgotten the wild escapade of Louis. He had no confidant whatever, not even a valet or a steward, and his most intimate associate knew nothing of his dark and secret counsels. When any one mentioned the ungovernable youth who had fled from the Hall, Lord Winterbourne said, "Pooh, pooh—he will soon discover his mistake," and smiled his pale and sinister smile. Such a face as his could not well look benign; but people were accustomed to his face, and thought it his misfortune—and everybody set him down as, in this instance at least, of a very forgiving and indulgent spirit, willing that the lad should find out his weakness by experiment, but not at all disposed to inflict any punishment upon his unruly son.

The fact was, however, that Lord Winterbourne was considerably excited and uneasy. He spent hours in a little private library among his papers—carefully went over them, collating and arranging again and again—destroyed some, and filled the private drawers of his cabinet with others. He sent orders to his agent to prosecute with all the energy possible his suit against the Athelings. He had his letters brought to him in his own room, where he was alone, and looked over them with eager haste and something like apprehension. Servants, always sufficiently quick-witted under such circumstances, concluded that my lord expected something, and the expectation descended accordingly through all the grades of the great house; but this did not by any means diminish the number of his guests, or the splendour of his hospitality. New arrivals came constantly to the Hall— and very great people indeed, on their way to Scotland and the moors, looked in upon the disappointed statesman by way of solace. He had made an unspeakable failure in his attempt at statesmanship; but still he had a certain amount of influence, and merited a certain degree of consideration. The quiet country brightened under the shower of noble sportsmen and fair ladies. All Banburyshire crowded to pay its homage. Mrs Edgerley brought her own private menagerie, the newest lion who could be heard of; and herself fell into the wildest fever of architecturalism—fitted up an oratory under the directions of a Fellow of Merton—set up an Ecclesiological Society in the darkest of her drawing-rooms—made drawings of "severe saints," and purchased casts of the finest "examples"—began to embroider an altar-cloth from the designs of one of the most renowned connoisseurs in the ecclesiological city, and talked of nothing but Early English, and Middle Pointed. Politics, literature, and the fine arts, sport, flirtation, and festivity, kept in unusual excitement the whole spectator county of Banbury, and the busy occupants of Winterbourne Hall.

In the midst of all this, the Lord of Winterbourne spent solitary hours in his library among his papers, took solitary rides towards Abingford, moodily courted a meeting with Miss Anastasia, even addressed her when they met, and did all that one unassisted man could do to gain information of her proceedings. He was in a state of restless expectation, not easy to account for. He knew that Louis was in London, but not who had given him the means to go there; and he could find no pretence for bringing back the youth, or asserting authority over him. He waited in well-concealed but frightfully-felt excitement for *something*, watching with a stealthy but perpetual observation the humble house of the Athelings and the Priory at Abingford. He did not say to himself what it was he apprehended, nor indeed that he apprehended anything; but with that strange certainty which criminals always seem to retain, that fate must come some time, waited in the midst of his gay, busy, frivolous guests, sharing all the occupations round him, like a man in a dream,—waited as the world waits in a pause of deadly silence for the thunderclap. It would rouse him when it came.

It came, but not as he looked for it. Oh blind, vain, guilty soul, with but one honest thought among all its crafts and falsehoods! It came not like the rousing tumult of the thunder, but like an avalanche from the hills; he fell under it with a groan of mortal agony; there was nothing in heaven or earth to defend him from the misery of this sudden blow. All his schemes, all his endeavours, what were they good for now?

CHAPTER VIII
THE NEW HEIR

They had heard from Charlie, who had already set out upon his journey; they had heard from Louis, whom Mr Foggo desired to take into his office in Charlie's place in the mean time; they had heard again and again from Miss Anastasia's solicitor, touching their threatened property; and to this whole family of women everything around seemed going on with a singular speed and bustle, while they, unwillingly detained among the waning September trees, were, by themselves, so lonely and so still. The only one among them who was not eager to go home was Agnes. Bellevue and Islington, though they were kindly enough in their way, were not meet nurses for a poetic child;—this time of mountainous clouds, of wistful winds, of falling leaves, was like a new life to Agnes. She came out to stand in the edge of the wood alone, to do nothing but listen to the sweep of the wild minstrel in those thinning trees, or look upon the big masses of cloud breaking up into vast shapes of windy gloom over the spires of the city and the mazes of the river. The great space before and around—the great amphitheatre at her feet—the breeze that came in her face fresh and chill, and touched with rain—the miracles of tiny moss and herbage lying low beneath those fallen leaves—the pale autumn sky, so dark and stormy—the autumn winds, which wailed o' nights—the picturesque and many-featured change which stole over everything—carried a new and strange delight to the mind of Agnes. She alone cared to wander by herself through the wood, with its crushed ferns, its piled faggots of firewood, its yellow leaves, which every breeze stripped down. She was busy with the new book, too, which was very like to be wanted before it came; for all these expenses, and the license which their supposed wealth had given them, had already very much reduced the little store of five-pound notes, kept for safety in Papa's desk.

One afternoon during this time of suspense and uncertainty, the Rector repeated his call at the Lodge. The Rector had never forgiven Agnes that unfortunate revelation of her authorship; yet he had looked to her notwithstanding through those strange sermons of his, with a constantly-increasing appeal to her attention. She was almost disposed to fancy sometimes that he made special fiery defences of himself and his sentiments, which seemed addressed to her only; and Agnes fled from the idea with distress and embarrassment, thinking it a vanity of her own. On this day, however, the Rector was a different man—the cloud was off his brow— the apparent restraint, uneasy and galling, under which he had seemed to hold himself, was removed; a flash of aroused spirit was in his eye—his very step was eager, and sounded with a bolder ring upon the gravel of the garden path—there was no longer the parochial bow, the clergymanly address, or the restless consciousness of something unreal in both, which once characterised him; he entered among them almost abruptly, and did not say a word of his parishioners, but instead, asked for Louis—told Rachel his sister wished to see her—and, glancing with unconcealed dislike at poor Agnes's blotting-book, wished to know if Miss Atheling was writing now.

"Mr Rivers does not think it right, mamma," said Agnes. She blushed a little under her consciousness of his look of displeasure, but smiled also with a kind of challenge as she met his eye.

"No," said the young clergyman abruptly; "I admire, above all things, understanding and intelligence. I can suppose no appreciation so quick and entire as a woman's; but she fails of her natural standing to me, when I come to hear of her productions, and am constituted a critic—that is a false relationship between a woman and a man."

And Mr Rivers looked at Agnes with an answering flash of pique and offence, which was as much as to say, "I am very much annoyed; I had thought of very different relationships; and it is all owing to you."

"Many very good critics," said Mrs Atheling, piqued in her turn—"a great many people, I assure you, who know about such things, have been very much pleased with Agnes's book."

The Rector made no answer—did not even make a pause—but as if all this was merely irrelevant and an interruption to his real business, said rapidly, yet with some solemnity, and without a word of preface, "Lord Winterbourne's son is dead."

"Who?" said Agnes, whom, unconsciously, he was addressing—and they all turned to him with a little anxiety. Rachel became very pale, and even Marian, who was not thinking at all of what Mr Rivers said, drew a little nearer the table, and looked up at him wistfully, with her beautiful eyes.

"Lord Winterbourne's son, George Rivers, the heir of the family— he who has been abroad so long; a young man, I hear, whom every one esteemed," said the Rector, bending down his head, as if he exacted from himself a certain sadness, and did indeed endeavour to see how sad it was—"he is dead."

Mrs Atheling rose, greatly moved. "Oh, Mr Rivers!—did you say his son? his only son? a young man? Oh, I pray God have pity upon him! It will kill him;—it will be more than he can bear!"

The Rector looked up at the grief in the good mother's face, with a look and gesture of surprise. "I never heard any one give Lord Winterbourne credit for so much feeling," he said, looking at her with some suspicion; "and surely he has not shown much of it to you."

"Oh, feeling! don't speak of feeling!" cried Mrs Atheling. "It is not that I am thinking of. You know a great many things, Mr Rivers, but you never lost a child."

"No," he said; and then, after a pause, he added, in a lower tone, "in the whole matter, certainly, I never before thought of Lord Winterbourne."

And there was nobody nigh to point out to him what a world beyond and above his philosophy was this simple woman's burst of nature. Yet in his own mind he caught a moment's glimpse of it; for the instant he was abashed, and bent his lofty head with involuntary self-humiliation; but looking up, saw his own thought still clearer in the eye of Agnes, and turned defiant upon her, as if it had been a spoken reproof.

"Well!" he said, turning to her, "was I to blame for thinking little of the possibility of grief in such a man?"

"I did not say so," said Agnes, simply; but she looked awed and grave, as the others did. They had no personal interest at all in the matter; they thought in an instant of the vacant places in their own family, and stood silent and sorrowful, looking at the great calamity which made another house desolate. They never thought of Lord Winterbourne, who was their enemy; they only thought of a father who had lost his son.

And Rachel, who remembered George Rivers, and thought in the tenderness of the moment that he had been rather kind to her, wept a few tears silently.

All these things disconcerted the Rector. He was impatient of excess of sympathy—ebullitions of feeling; he was conscious of a restrained, yet intense spring of new hope and vigour in his own life. He had endeavoured conscientiously to regret his cousin; but it was impossible to banish from his own mind the thought that he was free—that a new world opened to his ambition—that he was the heir!

And he had come, unaware of his own motive, to share this overpowering and triumphant thought with Agnes Atheling, a girl who was no mate for him, as inferior in family fortune and breeding as it was possible to imagine—and now stood abashed and reproved to see that all his simple auditors thought at once, not of him and his altered position, but of those grand and primitive realities—Death and Grief. He went away hastily and with impatience, displeased with them and with himself—went away on a rapid walk for miles out of his way, striding along the quiet country roads as if for a race; and a race it was, with his own thoughts, which still were fastest, and not to be overtaken. He knew the truths of philosophy, the limited lines and parallels of human logic and reason; but he had not been trained among the great original truths of nature; he knew only what was true to the mind,—not what was true to the heart.

CHAPTER IX
A VISIT

"Come down, Agnes, make haste; mamma wants you—and Miss Anastasia's carriage is just driving up to the door."

So said Marian, coming languidly into their sleeping-room, and quite indifferent to Miss Anastasia. She was rather glad indeed to hasten Agnes away, to make an excuse for herself, and gain a half-hour of solitude to read over again Louis's letter. It was worth while to get letters like those of Louis. Marian sat down on one of Miss Bridget's old-fashioned chairs, and leaned her beautiful head against its high unyielding angular back. The cover on it was of an ancient blue-striped tabinet, faded, yet still retaining some of its colour, which answered very well to relieve those beautiful half-curled, half-braided locks of Marian's hair, which had such a tendency to escape from all kinds of bondage. She lay there half reclining upon this stiff uneasy piece of furniture, not at all disturbed by its angularity, her pretty cheek flushing, her pretty lips trembling into half-conscious smiles, reading over again Louis's letter, which she held after an embracing fashion in both her hands.

And Rachel, with great diffidence, yet by the Rector's invitation, had gone to visit Miss Rivers at the Old Wood House. When the other Miss Rivers, chief of the name, entered the little parlour of the Lodge, she found the mother and daughter, who were both acquainted with her secret, awaiting her very anxiously. She came in with a grave face and deliberate step. She had not changed her dress in any particular, except the colour of her bonnet, which was black, and had some woeful decorations of crape; but it was evident that she too had been greatly moved and impressed by her young cousin's death.

"He is dead," she said, almost as abruptly as the Rector, when she had taken her usual place. "Yes, poor young George Rivers, who was the heir of the house—it was very well for him that he should die."

"Oh, Miss Rivers!" said Mrs Atheling, "I am very, very sorry for poor Lord Winterbourne."

"Are you?" said Miss Anastasia;—"perhaps you are right,—he will feel this, I dare say, as much as he can feel anything—but *I* was sorry for the boy. Young people think it hard to die—fools!—they don't know the blessing that lies in it. Living long enough to come to the crown of youth, and dying in its blossom—that's a lot fit for an angel. Agnes Atheling, never look through your tears at me."

But Agnes could not help looking at the old lady wistfully, with her young inquiring eyes.

"What does the Rector do here?—they tell me he comes often," said Miss Rivers. "Do you know that now, so far as people understand, *he* comes to be heir of Winterbourne?"

"He came to tell us yesterday of the poor young gentleman's death," said Mrs Atheling, "and I thought he seemed a little excited. Agnes, I am sure you observed it as well as I."

"No, mamma," said Agnes, turning away hastily. She went to get some work, that no one might observe her own looks, with a sudden nervous tremor and impatience upon her. The Rector had been very kind to Louis, had done a brother's part to him—far more than any one else in the world had ever done to this friendless youth—yet Louis's friends were labouring with all their might, working in darkness like evil-doers, to undermine the supposed right of Lionel—that right which made his breast expand and his brow clear, and freed him from an uncongenial fate. Agnes sat down trembling, with a sudden nervous access of vexation, disappointment, annoyance, which she could not explain. She had been accustomed for a long time now to follow him with interest and sympathy, and to read his thoughts in those wild public self-revelations of his, which no one penetrated but herself; but she felt actually guilty, a plotter, and concerned against him now.

"I am sorry for Lionel," said Miss Rivers, who had not lost a single fluctuation of colour on Agnes's cheek, nor tremble of emotion in her hurried hands—"but it would have been more grievous for poor George had he lived. There will be only disappointment—not disgrace—for any other heir."

She paused awhile, still watching Agnes, who bent over her work, greatly disposed to cry, and in a very agitated condition of mind. Then she said as suddenly as before, "I forget my proper errand—I have come for the girls. You are to go up with me to the Priory. Go, make haste—put on your bonnet—I never wait, even for young ladies; call your sister, and make ready to go."

Agnes rose, startled and unwilling, and cast an inquiring look at Mamma. Mrs Atheling was startled too, but she was not insensible to the pride and glory of seeing her two daughters drive off to Abingford Priory in the well-known carriage of Miss Anastasia. "Since Miss Rivers is so good, make haste, my dear," said Mrs Atheling; and Agnes had no alternative but to obey.

When she was gone, Miss Rivers looked round the room inquisitively. Rachel was no great needlewoman, nor much instructed in ordinary feminine pursuits; there were no visible traces of the presence of a third young lady in the little dim parlour. "Where is the girl?" said Miss Anastasia, cautiously,—"I was told she was here."

"The Rector asked her to go and see his sister—she is at the Old Wood House," said Mrs Atheling. "I am very sorry—but we never thought of you coming to-day."

"I might come any day," said Miss Rivers, abruptly—"but that is not the question—I prefer not to see her—she is a frightened little dove of a girl—she is not in my way. Is she good for anything?—you ought to know."

"She is a very sweet, amiable girl," said Mrs Atheling, warmly—"and she sings as I never heard any one sing, all my life."

"Ah!" said Miss Rivers, with a look of gratification, "it belongs to the family—music is a tradition among us—yes, yes! You remember my great-grandfather, the fourth lord—he was a great composer." Miss Anastasia was perfectly destitute of the faculty herself, and more than half of the Riverses wanted that humblest of all musical qualifications, "an ear"—yet it was amusing to mark the eagerness of the old lady to find a family precedent for every quality known as belonging to Louis or his sister. "I recollect," added Miss Rivers, bending her brows darkly, "they wanted to make a singer of her—the more disgrace the better—Oh, I understand their tactics! You are sorry for him?—look at the devilish plans he made."

Mrs Atheling shook her head, but did not reply; she only knew that she would have been sorry for the vilest criminal in the world, had he lost his only son.

"I have heard from your boy," said Miss Rivers. "He is gone now, I suppose. What does Will Atheling think of his son? If he does but as I expect he will, the boy's fortune is made; he shall never repent that he did this service for me."

"But it is a great undertaking," said Mrs Atheling. "I know Charlie will do his best—he is a very good boy, Miss Rivers; but he may not succeed after all."

"He will succeed," said the old lady; "but even if he does not—which I cannot believe—so long as he does all he can, it will not alter me."

The mother's heart swelled high with gratification and pleasure; yet there was a drawback. All this time—since the first day when she heard of it, before she made her discovery—Miss Anastasia had never referred to the engagement between Louis and Marian. Did she desire to discourage it? Was she likely to perceive a difference in this respect between Louis nameless and without friends, and Louis the heir of Winterbourne?

But Mrs Atheling's utmost penetration could not tell. Miss Rivers began to pull down the books, to look at them, to strike her riding-whip on the floor, and call out good-humouredly in her loud voice, which every one in the house could hear, that she was not to be kept waiting by a parcel of girls. Finally the girls made their appearance in their best dresses; their new patroness hurried them into her carriage, and drove instantly away.

CHAPTER X
MARIAN ON TRIAL

Miss Anastasia "preferred not to see" Rachel—yet, with a wayward inclination still, was moved to drive by a circuitous road in front of the Old Wood House, where the girl was. The little vehicle went heavily along the grassy road, cutting the turf, but making little sound as it rolled past the windows of the invalid. There was the velvet lawn, the trim flower-plots, the tall autumnal flowers, the straight and well-kept garden-paths, lying vacant and shadowless beneath the sun—but there was nothing to be discovered under the closed blinds of this shut-up and secluded house.

"Why do they keep their blinds down?" said Miss Anastasia; "all the house surely is not one invalid's room? Lucy was a little fool always. I do not believe there is anything the matter with her. She had what these soft creatures call a disappointment in love—words have different meanings, child. And why does this girl go to see Lucy Rivers? I suppose because she is such a one herself."

"It is because Miss Rivers was kind to her," said Agnes; "and the Rector asked her to go——"

"The Rector? Do you mean to tell me," said Miss Anastasia, turning quickly upon her companion, "that when Lionel Rivers comes to the Lodge it is for *her* he comes?"

"I do not know," said Agnes. She was provoked to feel how her face burned under the old lady's gaze. She could not help showing something of the anger and vexation she felt. She looked up hastily, with a glance of resentment. "He has been very much interested in Louis—he has been very kind to him," said Agnes, not at all indisposed, for the sake of the Rector, whom every one plotted against, to throw down her glove to Miss Anastasia. "I believe, indeed, it has been to inquire about Louis, that he ever came to the Lodge."

Miss Anastasia touched her ponies with her whip, and said, "Humph!" "Both of them! odd enough," said the old lady. Agnes, who was considerably offended, and not at all in an amicable state of mind, did not choose to inquire who Miss Anastasia meant by "both of them," nor what it was that was "odd enough."

Marian occupied the seat behind. She liked it very well, though she would rather have written her letter to Louis. She did not quite hear the conversation before her, and did not much care about it. Marian recognised the old lady only as Agnes's friend, and had never connected her in any way with her own fortunes. She was shy of speaking in that stately presence; she was even resentful sometimes of the remarks of Miss Anastasia; and the lofty old gentlewoman had formed but an indifferent idea yet of the little beauty. She was amused with the pretty pout of Marian's lip, the sparkle, sometimes of fun, sometimes of petulance, in her eye; but Marian would have been extremely dismayed to-day had she known that she, and not Agnes, was the principal object of Miss Anastasia's visit, and was, indeed, about to be put upon her trial, to see if she was good for anything. At all events, she was quite at ease and unalarmed now.

They drove along in silence for some time after this—passing through the village and past the Park gates. Then Miss Anastasia took a road quite unfamiliar to the girls—a grass-grown unfrequented path, lying under the shadow of the trees of Winterbourne. She did not say a word till they came to a sudden break in the trees, when she stopped her ponies abruptly, and fixed a sorrowful gaze upon the Hall, which was visible, and close at hand. The white, broad, majestic front of the great house was not unlike a funeral pile at any time; now, with white curtains drawn close over all its scarcely perceptible windows, still veiled in the pomp of mourning, without a gleam of light or colour, in its blind, grand aspect, turning its back upon the sun— there was something very sadly imposing in the desolated house. No one was to be seen about it—not even a servant: it looked like a vast mausoleum, sacred to the dead. "It was very well for him," said Miss Anastasia with a sigh, "very well. If it were not so pitiful a thing to think of, children, I could thank God."

But as the old lady spoke, the tears stood heavy in her eyes.

This was very dreadful, very mysterious, altogether beyond comprehension to Marian. She was glad to turn her eyes away from the house with dislike and terror—it had been Louis's prison and place of suffering, and not a single hope connected with the Hall of Winterbourne was in Marian's mind. She drew back from Miss Rivers with a shudder—she thought it was the most frightful thing in existence to thank God because this young man had died.

The Priory opened its doors wide to its mistress and her young guests. She led them herself to her favourite room, a very strange place, indeed, to their inexperienced eyes. It was a long narrow room, built over the archway which crossed the entrance to the town of Abingford. This of itself was peculiarity enough; and the walls were of stone, wainscoted to half their height with oak, and the roof was ribbed with strong old oaken rafters, and of course unceiled. Windows on either side, plain lattice-windows, with thick mullions of stone, admitted the light in strips between heavy bars of shadow, and commanded a full sight of every one who entered the town of Abingford. On the country side was a long country road, some trees, and the pale convolutions of the river; on the other, there was a glimpse of the market-place of the town, even now astir with a leisurely amount of business, in the centre of which rose an extraordinary building with a piazza, while round it were the best shops of Abingford, and the farmers' inns, which were full on market days. A little old church, rich with the same rude Saxon ornament which decorated the church of Winterbourne, stood modestly among the houses at the corner of the market-place. A few leisurely figures, such as belong to country towns, stood at the doors, or lounged about the pavement; and market-carts came and went slowly under the arch. Marian brightened into positive amusement; she thought it very funny indeed to watch the people and the vehicles slowly disappearing beneath her, and laughed to herself, and thought it a very odd fancy of Miss Anastasia, to choose her favourite sitting-room here.

The old lady came and stood beside her, somewhat to the embarrassment of Marian. She bade the girl take off her bonnet, which produced its unfailing result, of throwing into a little picturesque confusion those soft, silken, half-curled tresses of Marian's hair. Marian looked out of the window somewhat nervously, a little afraid of Miss Rivers. The old lady looked at her with a keen scrutiny. She was stooping her pretty shoulders in an attitude which might have been awkward in a form less elastic, dimpling her cheek with the fingers which supported it, conscious of Miss Anastasia's gaze, somewhat alarmed, and very shy. In spite of the shrinking, the alarm, and the embarrassment, Miss Rivers looked steadily down upon her with a serious inspection. But even the cloud which began to steal over Marian's brow could not disenchant the eyes that gazed upon her—Miss Anastasia began to smile as everybody else; to feel herself moved to affection, tenderness, regard; to own the fascination which no one resisted. "My dear, you are very pretty," said the old lady, entirely forgetting any prudent precautions on the score of making Marian vain; "many people would tell you, that, with a face like that, you need no other attraction. But I was once pretty myself, and I know it does not last for ever; do you ever think about anything, you lovely little child?"

Marian glanced up with an indignant blush and frown; but the look she met was so kind, that it was not possible to answer as she intended. So the pretty head sank down again upon the hand which supported it. She took a little time to compose herself, and then, with some humility, spoke the truth: "I am afraid, not a great deal."

"What do you suppose I do here, all by myself?" said Miss Anastasia, suddenly.

Marian turned her face towards her, looked round the room, and then turned a wistful gaze to Miss Rivers. "Indeed, I do not know," said Marian, in a very low and troubled tone: it was youth, with awe and gravity and pity, looking out of its bright world upon the loneliness and poverty of age.

That answer and that look brought the examination to a very hasty and sudden conclusion. The old lady looked at her for an instant with a startled glance, stooped over her, kissed her forehead and hurried away. Marian could not tell what she had done, nor why Miss Anastasia's face changed so strangely. She could not comprehend the full force of the contrast, nor how her own simple wonder and pity struck like a sudden arrow to the old lady's heart.

Agnes was puzzled too, and could not help her sister to an explanation. They remained by themselves for some time, rather timidly looking at everything. There were a few portraits hanging high upon the walls, portraits which they knew to be of the family, but could not recognise; and there was one picture of a very strange kind, which all their combined ingenuity could not interpret. It was like one of those old Dyptichs used to preserve some rare and precious altarpiece. What was within could not be seen, but on the closed leaves without were painted two solemn angels, with a silvery surrounding of wings, and flowers in their hands. If Miss Anastasia had been a Catholic—even if she had been a dilettante or extreme High Churchwoman, it might have been a little private shrine: perhaps it was so: there was a portrait within, which no eyes but her own ever saw. Between the windows the walls were lined with book-cases; that ancient joke of poor Aunt Bridget's, her own initials underneath her pupil's name—the B. A., which conferred a degree upon Anastasia Rivers—turned out to be an intentional thing after all. The girls gazed in awe at Miss Anastasia's book-shelves. She was a great scholar, this old lady. She might have been one of the Heads of Houses in the learned city, but for the unfortunate femininity which debarred her. All by herself among these tomes of grey antiquity—all by herself with her pictures, the sole remnant of another time—it was not wonderful that the two girls paused, looking out from the sunshine of their youth with reverence, yet with compassion. They honoured her with natural humility, feeling their own ignorance, but notwithstanding, were very sorry for Miss Anastasia, all by herself—more sorry than there was occasion to be—for Miss Anastasia was used to be all by herself, and found enjoyment in it now.

When Miss Anastasia came back she took them to see her garden, and the state-apartments of her great stately house. When they were a little familiar she let them stray on before her, and followed watching. Agnes, perhaps, was still her own favourite of the two; but all her observation was given to Marian. As her eyes followed this beautiful figure, her look became more and more satisfied; and while Marian wandered with her sister about the garden, altogether unconscious of the great possibilities which awaited her, Miss Anastasia's fancy clothed her in robes of state, and covered her with jewels. "He might have married a duke's daughter," she said to herself, turning away with a pleased eye—"but he might never have found such a beautiful fairy as this: she is a good little child too, with no harm in her; and a face for a fairy queen!"

CHAPTER XI
DISCONTENT

No one knew the real effect of the blow which had just fallen upon Lord Winterbourne. The guests, of whom his house was full, dispersed as if by magic. Even Mrs Edgerley, in the most fashionable sables, with mourning liveries, and the blinds of her carriage solemnly let down, went forth, as soon as decency would permit, from the melancholy Hall. After all the bustle and all the gaiety of recent days, the place fell into a pause of deadly stillness. Lord Winterbourne sought comfort from no one—showed grief to no one; he made a sudden pause, like a man stunned, and then, with increased impetus, and with a force and resolution unusual to him, resumed his ancient way once more, and rushed forward with exaggerated activity. Instead of subduing him, this event seemed to have roused all his faculties into a feverish and busy malevolence, as if the man had said, "I have no one to come after me—I will do all the harm I can while my time lasts." All the other gentry of the midland counties, put together, did not bring so many poachers to "justice" as were brought by Lord Winterbourne. It was with difficulty his solicitor persuaded him to pass over the pettiest trespass upon his property. He shut up pathways privileged from time immemorial, ejected poor tenants, encroached upon the village rights, and oppressed the village patriarchs; and animated as he was by this spirit of ill-will to every one, it was not wonderful that he endeavoured, with all his might, to press on the suit against the Athelings for the recovery of the Old Wood Lodge.

Mrs Atheling and her daughters, unwilling, embarrassed, and totally ignorant of their real means of defence, remained in their house at the pleasure of the lawyer, and much against their own inclination. Mrs Atheling herself, though with a spark of native spirit she had seconded her husband's resolution not to give up his little inheritance, was entirely worried out with the task of defending it, now that Charlie was gone, and winter was approaching, and her heart yearned to her husband and her forsaken house in Bellevue. When she wrote to Mr Atheling, or when she consulted with Agnes, the good mother expressed her opinion very strongly. "If it turns out a mistake about Louis, none of us will care for this place," said Mrs Atheling; "we shall have the expense of keeping it up, and unless we were living in it ourselves, I do not suppose it is worth ten pounds a-year; and if it should turn out true about Louis, of course he would restore it to us, and settle it so that there could be no doubt upon the subject; and indeed, Agnes, my dear, the only sensible plan that I can think of, would be to give it up at once, and go home. I do think it is quite an unfortunate house for the Athelings; there was your father's poor little sister got her death in it; and it is easy to see how much trouble and anxiety have come into our family since we came here."

"But trouble and anxiety might come anywhere, mamma," said Agnes.

"Yes, my dear, that is very true; but we should have known exactly what we had to look for, if Marian had been engaged to some one in Bellevue."

Mamma's counsels, accordingly, were of a very timid and compromising character. She began to be extremely afraid that the Old Wood Lodge, being so near the trees, would be damp after all the autumn rains, and that something might possibly happen to Bell and Beau; and, with all her heart, and without any dispute, she longed exceedingly to be at home. Then there was the pretty pensive Marian, a little love-sick, and pining much for the society of her betrothed. She was a quiet but potent influence, doing what she could to aggravate the discontent of Mamma; and Agnes had to keep up the family courage, and develop the family patience, single-handed. Agnes, in her own private heart, though she did not acknowledge, nor even know it, was not at all desirous to go away.

The conflict accordingly, about this small disputed possession, lay a great deal more between Lord Winterbourne and Miss Anastasia than between that unfriendly nobleman and the house of Atheling. Miss Anastasia came frequently on errands of encouragement to fortify the sinking heart of Mrs Atheling. "My great object is to defer the trial of this matter for six months," said the old lady significantly. "Let it come on, and we will turn the tables then."

She spoke in the presence of Marian, before whom nothing could be said plainly—in the presence of Rachel even, whom it was impossible to avoid seeing, but who always kept timidly in the background—and she spoke with a certain exultation which somewhat puzzled her auditors. Charlie, though he had done nothing yet, had arrived at the scene of his labours. Assured of this fact, the courage of his patroness rose. She was a woman and an optimist, as she confessed. She had the gift of leaping to a conclusion, equal to any girl in the kingdom, and at the present moment was not disturbed by any doubts of success.

"Six months!" cried Mrs Atheling, in dismay and horror; "and do you mean that we must stay here all that time—all the winter, Miss Rivers? It is quite impossible—indeed I could not do it. My husband is all by himself, and I know how much I am wanted at home."

"It is necessary some one should be in possession," said Miss Rivers. "Eh? What does Will Atheling say?—I daresay he thinks it hard enough to be left alone."

Mrs Atheling was very near "giving away." Vexation and anxiety for the moment almost overpowered her self-command. She knew all the buttons must be off Papa's shirts, and stood in grievous fear of a fabulous amount of broken crockery; besides, she had never been so long parted from her husband since their marriage, and very seriously longed for home.

"Of course it is very dreary for him," she said, with a sigh.

"Mr Temple is making application to defer the trial on the score of an important witness who cannot reach this country in time," said Miss Rivers. "Of course my lord will oppose that with all his power; *he* has a natural terror of witnesses from abroad. When the question is decided, I do not see, for my part, why you should remain. This little one pines to go home, I see—but you, Agnes Atheling, you had better come and stay at the Priory— you love the country, child!"

Both the sisters blushed under the scrutinising eye of Miss Anastasia; but Agnes was not yet reconciled to the old lady. "We are all anxious to go home," she said with spirit, and with considerably more earnestness than the case at all demanded. Miss Rivers smiled a little. She thought she could read a whole romance in the fluctuating colour and troubled glance of Agnes; but she was wrong, as far-seeing people are so often. The girl was disturbed, uneasy, self-conscious, in a startled and impatient condition of mind; but the romance, even if it were on the way, had not yet definitely begun.

CHAPTER XII
A CONVERSATION

Agnes's rambles out of doors had now almost always to be made alone. Rachel was much engrossed with the invalid of the Old Wood House, who had "taken a fancy" to the gentle little girl. The hypochondriac Miss Rivers was glad of any one so tender and respectful; and half in natural pity for the sufferings which Rachel could not believe to be fanciful, half from a natural vocation for kindly help and tendance, the girl was glad to respond to the partly selfish affection of her new friend, who told Rachel countless stories of the family, and the whole chronicle in every particular of her own early "disappointment in love." In return, Rachel, by snatches, conveyed to her invalid friend—in whom, after all, she found some points of interest and congeniality—a very exalted ideal picture of the Athelings, the genius of Agnes, and the love-story of Marian. Marian and Agnes occupied a very prominent place indeed in the talk of that shadowy dressing-room, with all its invalid contrivances—its closed green blinds, its soft mossy carpets, on which no footstep was ever audible, its easy little couches, which you could move with a finger; the luxury, and the stillness, and the gossip, were not at all unpleasant to Rachel; and she read *Hope Hazlewood* to her companion in little bits, with pauses of talk between. *Hope Hazlewood* was not nearly romantic enough for the pretty faded invalid reposing among her pillows in her white dressing-gown, whom Time seemed to have forgotten there, and who had no recollection for her own part that she was growing old; but she took all the delight of a girl in hearing of Louis and Marian—how much attached to each other, and how handsome they both were.

And Marian Atheling did not care half so much as she used to do for the long rambles with her sister, which were once such a pleasure to both the girls. Marian rather now preferred sitting by herself over her needlework, or lingering alone at the window, in an entire sweet idleness, full of all those charmed visions with which the very name of Louis peopled all the fairy future. Not the wisest, or the wittiest, or the most brilliant conversation in the world could have half equalled to Marian the dreamy pleasure of her own meditations. So Agnes had to go out alone.

Agnes did not suffer very much from this necessity. She wandered along the skirts of the wood, with a vague sense of freedom and enjoyment not easy to explain in words. No dreamy trance of magic influence had come upon Agnes; her mind, and her heart, and her thoughts, were quickened by a certain thrill of expectation, which was not to be referred to the strange romance now going on in the family—to Charlie's mission, nor Louis's prospects, nor anything else which was definite and ascertained. She knew that her heart rose, that her mind brightened, that her thoughts were restless and light, and not to be controlled; but she could not tell the reason why. She went about exploring all the country byways, and finding little tracks among the brushwood undiscoverable to the common eye; and she was not cogitating anything, scarcely was thinking, but somehow felt within her whole nature a silent growth and increase not to be explained.

She was pondering along, with her eyes upon the wide panorama at her feet, when it chanced to Agnes, suddenly and without preparation, to encounter the Rector. These two young people, who were mutually attracted to each other, had at the present moment a mutual occasion of embarrassment and apparent offence. The Rector could not forget how very much humbled in his own opinion he himself had been on his late visit to the Lodge; he had not yet recovered the singular check given to his own unconscious selfishness, by the natural sympathy of these simple people with the grander primitive afflictions and sufferings of life: and he was not without an idea that Agnes looked upon him now with a somewhat disdainful eye. Agnes, on her part, was greatly oppressed by the secret sense of being concerned against the Rector; in his presence she felt like a culprit—a secret plotter against the hope which brightened his eye, and expanded his mind. A look of trouble came at once into her face; her brow clouded—she thought it was not quite honest to make a show of friendship, while she retained her secret knowledge of the inquiry which might change into all the bitterness of disappointment his sudden and unlooked-for hope.

He had been going in the opposite direction, but, though he was not at all reconciled to her, he was not willing either to part with Agnes. He turned, only half consciously, only half willingly, yet by an irresistible compulsion. He tried indifferent conversation, and so did she; but, in spite of himself, Lionel Rivers was a truer man with Agnes Atheling than he was with any other person in the world. He who had never cared for sympathy from any one, somehow or other felt a necessity for hers, and had a certain imperious disappointment and impatience when it was withheld from him, which was entirely unreasonable, and not to be accounted for. He broke off abruptly from the talk about nothing, to speak of some intended movements of his own.

"I am going to town," said Mr Rivers. "I am somewhat unsettled at present in my intentions; after that, probably, I may spend some time abroad."

"All because he is the heir!" thought Agnes to herself; and again she coloured with distress and vexation. It was impossible to keep something of this from her tone; when she spoke, it was in a voice subdued a little out of its usual tenor; but all that she asked was a casual question, meaning nothing—"If Mr Mead would have the duty while the Rector was away?"

"Yes," said the Rector; "he is very much better fitted for it than I am. Here I have been cramping my wings these three years. Fathers and mothers are bitterly to blame; they bind a man to what his soul loathes, because it is his best method of earning some paltry pittance—so much a-year!"

After this exclamation the young clergyman made a pause, and so did his diffident and uneasy auditor, who "did not like" either to ask his meaning, or to make any comment upon it. After a few minutes he resumed again—

"I suppose it must constantly be so where we dare to think for ourselves," he said, in a tone of self-conversation. "A man who thinks *must* come to conclusions different from those which are taught to him—different, perhaps, from all that has been concluded truest in the ages that are past. What shall we say? Woe be to me if I do not follow out my reasoning, to whatever length it may lead!"

"When Paul says, Woe be to him, it is, if he does not preach the Gospel," said Agnes.

Mr Rivers smiled. "Be glad of your own happy exemption," he said, turning to her, with the air of a man who knows by heart all the old arguments—all the feminine family arguments against scepticism and dangerous speculations. "I will leave you in possession of your beautiful Gospel—your pure faith. I shall not attempt to disturb your mind—do not fear."

"You could not!" said Agnes, in a sudden and rash defiance. She turned to him in her turn, beginning to tremble a little with the excitement of controversy. She was a young polemic, rather more graceful in its manifestation, but quite as strong in the spirit of the conflict as any Mause Headrigg—which is to say, that, after her eager girlish fashion, she believed with her whole heart, and did not know what toleration meant.

Mr Rivers smiled once more. "I will not try," he said. "I remember what Christ said, and endeavour to have charity even for those who condemn me."

"Oh, Mr Rivers!" cried Agnes suddenly, and with trembling, "do not speak so coldly—do not say Christ; it sounds as if you did not care for Him—as if you thought He was no friend to you."

The Rector paused, somewhat startled: it was an objection which never had occurred to him—one of those subtle touches concerning the spirit and not the letter, which, being perfectly sudden, and quite simple, had some chance of coming to the heart.

"What do *you* say?" he asked with a little interest.

Agnes's voice was low, and trembled with reverence and with emotion. She was not thinking of him, in his maze of intellectual trifling—she was thinking of that Other, whom she knew so much better, and whose name she spoke. She answered with an involuntary bending of her head—"Our Lord."

It was no conviction that struck the mind of the young man—conviction was not like to come readily to him—and he was far too familiar with all the formal arguments, to be moved by the reasonings of a polemic, or the fervour of an enthusiast. But he who professed so much anxiety about truth, and contemplated himself as a moral martyr, woefully following his principles, though they led him to ever so dark a desolation, had lived all his life among an infinite number of shams, and willingly enough had yielded to many of them. Perhaps this was the first time in his life in which he had been brought into immediate contact with people who were simply true in their feelings and their actions—whose opinions were without controversy—whose settled place in life, humble as it was, shut them out from secondary emulations and ambitions—and who were swayed by the primitive rule of human existence—the labour and the rest, the affliction and the prosperity, which were real things, and not creations of the brain. He paused a little over the words of Agnes Atheling. He did not want her to think as he did: he was content to believe that the old boundaries were suitable and seemly for a woman; and he was rather pleased than otherwise, by the horror, interest, and regret which such opinions as his generally met with. He paused upon her words, with the air of a spectator, and said in a meditative fashion, "It is a glorious faith."

Now Agnes, who was not at all satisfied with this contemplative approval, was entirely ready and eager for controversy; prepared to plunge into it with the utmost rashness, utterly unaccoutred and ignorant as she was. She trembled with suppressed fervour and excitement over all her frame. She was as little a match for the Rector in the argument which she would fain have entered into, as any child in the village; but she was far too strong in the truth of her cause to feel any fear.

"Do you ever meet with great trouble?" said Agnes.

It was quite an unexpected question. The Rector looked at her inquiringly, without the least perception what she meant.

"And when you meet with it," continued the eager young champion, "what do you say?"

Now this was rather a difficult point with the Rector; it was not naturally his vocation to administer comfort to "great trouble"—in reality, when he was brought face to face with it, he had nothing to say. He paused a little, really embarrassed—*that* was the curate's share of the business. Mr Rivers was very sorry for the poor people, but had, in fact, no consolation to give, and thought it much more important to play with his own mind and faculties in this solemn and conscientious trifling of his, than to attend to the griefs of others. He answered, after some hesitation: "There are different minds, of course, and different influences applicable to them. Every man consoles himself after his own fashion; for some there are the sublime consolations of Philosophy, for others the rites of the Church."

"Some time," said Agnes suddenly, turning upon him with earnest eyes,—"some time, when you come upon great sorrow, will you try the name of our Lord?"

The young man was startled again, and made no answer. He was struck by the singular conviction that this girl, inferior to himself in every point, had a certain real and sublime acquaintance with that wonderful Person of whom she spoke; that this was by no means belief in a doctrine, but knowledge of a glorious and extraordinary Individual, whose history no unbeliever in the world has been able to divest of its original majesty. The idea was altogether new to him; it found an unaccustomed way to the heart of the speculatist—that dormant power which scarcely any one all his life had tried to reach to. "I do not quite understand you," he said somewhat moodily; but he did not attend to what she said afterwards. He pondered upon the problem by himself, and could not make anything of it. Arguments about doctrines and beliefs were patent enough to the young man. He was quite at home among dogmas and opinions—but, somehow, this personal view of the question had a strange advantage over him. He was not prepared for it; its entire and obvious simplicity took away the ground from under his feet. It might be easy enough to persuade a man out of conviction of a doctrine which he believed, but it was a different matter to disturb the identity of a person whom he knew.

CHAPTER XIII
SUSPENSE

In the mean time, immediate interest in their own occupations had pretty nearly departed from the inhabitants of the Old Wood Lodge. Agnes went on with her writing, Mamma with her work-basket, Marian with her dreams; but desk, and needle, and meditations were all alike abandoned in prospect of the postman, who was to be seen making his approach for a very long way, and was watched every day with universal anxiety. What Louis was doing, what Charlie was doing, the progress of the lawsuit, and the plans of Miss Anastasia, continually drew the thoughts of the household away from themselves. Even Rachel's constant report of the unseen invalid, Miss Lucy, added to the general withdrawal of interest from the world within to the world without. They seemed to have nothing to do themselves in their feminine quietness. Mamma sat pondering over her work—about her husband, who was alone, and did not like his solitude—about Charlie, who was intrusted with so great a commission—about "all the children"—every one of whom seemed to be getting afloat on a separate current of life. Agnes mused over her business with impatient thoughts about the Rector, with visions of Rachel and Miss Lucy in the invalid chamber, and vain attempts to look into the future and see what was to come. As for Marian, the charmed tenor of her fancies knew no alteration; she floated on, without interruption, in a sweet vision, full of a thousand consistencies, and wilder than any romance. Their conversation ran no longer in the ancient household channel, and was no more about their own daily occupations; they were spectators eagerly looking from the windows at nearly a dozen different conflicts, earnestly concerned, and deeply sympathetic, but not in the strife themselves.

Louis had entered Mr Foggo's office; it seemed a strange destination for the young man. He did not tell any one how small a remuneration he received for his labours, nor how he contrived to live in the little room, in the second floor of one of those Islington houses. He succeeded in existing—that was enough; and Louis did not chafe at his restrained and narrow life, by reason of having all his faculties engaged and urgent in a somewhat fanciful mode, of securing the knowledge which he longed for concerning his own birth and derivation. He had ascertained from Mr Atheling every particular concerning the Rivers family which *he* knew. He had even managed to seek out some old servants once at the Hall, and with a keen and intense patience had listened to every word of a hundred aimless and inconclusive stories from these respectable authorities. He was compiling, indeed, neither more nor less than a *life* of Lord Winterbourne—a history which he endeavoured to verify in every particular as he went on, and which was written with the sternest impartiality—a plain and clear record of events. Perhaps a more remarkable manuscript than that of Louis never existed; and he pursued his tale with all the zest, and much more than the excitement, of a romancer. It was a true story, of which he laboured to find out every episode; and there was a powerful unity and constructive force in the one sole unvarying interest of the tale. Mr Atheling had been moved to tell the eager youth *all* the particulars of his early acquaintance with Lord Winterbourne—and still the story grew—the object of the whole being to discover, as Louis himself said, "what child there was whom it was his interest to disgrace and defame." The young man followed hotly upon this clue. His thoughts had not been directed yet to anything resembling the discovery of Miss Anastasia; it had never occurred to him that his disinheritance might be absolutely the foundation of all Lord Winterbourne's greatness; but he hovered about the question with a singular pertinacity, and gave his full attention to it. Inspired by this, he did not consider his meagre meal, his means so narrow that it was the hardest matter in the world to eat daily bread. He pursued his story with a concentration of purpose which the greatest poet in existence might have envied. He was a great deal too much in earnest to think about the sentences in which he recorded what he learnt. The consequence was, that this memoir of Lord Winterbourne was a model of terse and pithy English— an unexampled piece of biography. Louis did not say a word about it to any one, but pursued his labour and his inquiry together, vainly endeavouring to find out a trace of some one whom he could identify with himself.

Meanwhile, Papa began to complain grievously of his long abandonment, and moved by Louis on one side, and by his own discomfort on the other, became very decided in his conviction that there was no due occasion for the absence of his family. There was great discontent in Number Ten, Bellevue, and there was an equal discontent, rather more overpowering, and quite as genuine, in the Old Wood Lodge, where Mamma and Marian vied with each other in anxiety, and thought no cause sufficiently important to keep them any longer from home. Agnes expressed no opinion either on one side or the other; she was herself somewhat disturbed and unsettled, thinking a great deal more about the Rector than was at all convenient, or to her advantage. After that piece of controversy, the Rector began to come rather often to the Lodge. He never said a word again touching that one brief breath of warfare, yet they eyed each other distrustfully, with a mutual consciousness of what had occurred, and might occur again. It was not a very lover-like point of union, yet it was a secret link of which no one else knew. Unconsciously it drew Agnes into inferences and implications, which were spoken at the Rector; and unconsciously it drew him to more sympathy with common trials, and a singular inclination to experiment, as Agnes had bidden him, with her sublime talisman—that sole Name given under heaven, which has power to touch into universal brotherhood the whole universal heart of man.

CHAPTER XIV
NEWS

While the Lodge remained in this ferment of suspense and uncertainty, Miss Anastasia had taken her measures for its defence and preservation. It was wearing now towards the end of October, and winter was setting in darkly. There was no more than a single rose at a time now upon the porch, and these roses looked so pale, pathetic, and solitary, that it was rather sad than pleasant to see the lonely flowers. On one of the darkest days of the month, when they were all rather more listless than usual, Miss Anastasia's well-known equipage drew up at the gate. They all hailed it with some pleasure. It was an event in the dull day and discouraging atmosphere. She came in with her loud cheerful voice, her firm step, her energetic bearing—and even the pretty *fiancée* Marian raised her pretty stooping shoulders, and woke up from her fascinated musing. Rachel alone drew shyly towards the door; she had not overcome a timidity very nearly approaching fear, which she always felt in presence of Miss Anastasia. She was the only person who ever entered this house who made Rachel remember again her life at the Hall.

"I came to show you a letter from your boy; read it while I talk to the children," said Miss Rivers. Mrs Atheling took the letter with some nervousness; she was a little fluttered, and lost the sense of many of the expressions; yet lingered over it, notwithstanding, with pride and exultation. She longed very much to have an opportunity of showing it to Agnes; but that was not possible; so Mrs Atheling made a virtuous attempt to preserve in her memory every word that her son said. This was Charlie's letter to his patroness:—

"Madam,—I have not made very much progress yet. The courier, Jean Monte, is to be heard of as you suggested; but it is only known on the road that he lives in Switzerland, and keeps some sort of inn in one of the mountain villages. No more as yet; but I will find him out. I have to be very cautious at present, because I am not yet well up in the language. The town is a ruinous place, and I cannot get the parish registers examined as one might do in England. There are several families of decayed nobles in the immediate neighbourhood, and, so far as I can hear, Giulietta is a very common name. Travelling Englishmen, too, are so frequent that there is a good deal of difficulty. I am rather inclined to fix upon the villa Remori, where there are said to have been several English marriages. It has been an extensive place, but is now broken down, decayed, and neglected; the family have a title, and are said to be very handsome, but are evidently very poor. There is a mother and a number of daughters, only one or two grown up; I try to make acquaintance with the children. The father died early, and had no brothers. I think possibly this might be the house of Giulietta, as there is no one surviving to look after the rights of her children, did she really belong to this family. Of course, any relatives she had, with any discretion, would have inquired out her son in England; so I incline to think she may have belonged to the villa Remori, as there are only women there.

"I have to be very slow on account of my Italian—this, however, remedies itself every day. I shall not think of looking for Monte till I have finished my business here, and am on my way home. The place is unprosperous and unhealthy, but it is pretty, and rather out of the way—few travellers came, they tell me, till within ten years ago; but I have not met with any one yet whose memory carried back at all clearly for twenty years. A good way out of the town, near the lake, there is a kind of mausoleum which interests me a little, not at all unlike the family tomb at Winterbourne; there is no name upon it; it lies quite out of the way, and I cannot ascertain that any one has ever been buried there; but something may be learned about it, perhaps, by-and-by.

"When I ascertain anything of the least importance, I shall write again.

"Madam,
"Your obedient Servant,
"Charles Atheling."

Charlie had never written to a lady before; he was a little embarrassed about it the first time, but this was his second epistle, and he had become a little more at his ease. The odd thing about the correspondence was, that Charlie did not express either hopes or opinions; he did not say what he expected, or what were his chances of success—he only reported what he was doing; any speculation upon the subject, more especially at this crisis, would have been out of Charlie's way.

"What do you call your brother when you write to him?" asked Miss Anastasia abruptly, addressing Rachel.

Rachel coloured violently; she had so nearly forgotten her old system—her old representative character—that she was scarcely prepared to answer such a question. With a mixture of her natural manner and her assumed one, she answered at last, in considerable confusion, "We call him Louis; he has no other name."

"Then he will not take the name of Rivers?" said Miss Anastasia, looking earnestly at the shrinking girl.

"We have no right to the name of Rivers," said Rachel, drawing herself up with her old dignity, like a little queen. "My brother is inquiring who we are. We never belonged to Lord Winterbourne."

"Your brother is inquiring? So!" said Miss Anastasia; "and he is perfectly right. Listen, child—tell him this from me—do you know what Atheling means? It means noble, illustrious, royally born. In the old Saxon days the princes were called Atheling. Tell your brother that Anastasia Rivers bids him bear this name."

This address entirely confused Rachel, who remained gazing at Miss Rivers blankly, unable to say anything. Marian stirred upon her chair with sudden eagerness, and put down her needlework, gazing also, but after quite a different fashion, in Miss Anastasia's face. The old lady caught the look of both, but only replied to the last.

"You are startled, are you, little beauty? Did you never hear the story of Margaret Atheling, who was an exile, and a saint, and a queen? My child, I should be very glad to make sure that you were a true Atheling too."

Marian was not to be diverted from her curiosity by any such observation. She cast a quick look from Miss Rivers to her mother, who was pondering over Charlie's letter, and from Mrs Atheling to Agnes, who had not been startled by the strange words of Miss Anastasia; and suspicion, vague and unexplainable, began to dawn in Marian's mind.

"The autumn assizes begin to-day," said Miss Anastasia with a little triumph; "too soon, as Mr Temple managed it, for your case to have a hearing; it must stand over till the spring now—six months—by that time, please God; we shall be ready for them. Agnes Atheling, how long is it since you began to be deaf and blind?"

Agnes started with a little confusion, and made a hurried inarticulate answer. There was a little quiet quarrel all this time going on between Agnes and Miss Rivers; neither the elder lady nor the younger was quite satisfied — Agnes feeling herself something like a conspirator, and Miss Anastasia a little suspicious of her, as a disaffected person in the interest of the enemy. But Mamma by this time had come to an end of Charlie's letter, and, folding it up very slowly, gave it back to its proprietor. The good mother did not feel it at all comfortable to keep this information altogether to herself.

"It is not to be tried till spring!" said Mrs Atheling, who had caught this observation. "Then, I think, indeed, Miss Rivers, we must go home."

And, to Mamma's great comfort, Miss Anastasia made no objection. She said kindly that she should miss her pleasant neighbours. "But what may be in the future, girls, no one knows," said Miss Rivers, getting up abruptly. "Now, however, before this storm comes on, I am going home."

CHAPTER XV
GOING HOME

After this the family made immediate preparations for their return. Upon this matter Rachel was extremely uncomfortable, and much divided in her wishes. Miss Lucy, who had been greatly solaced by the gentle ministrations of this mild little girl, insisted very much that Rachel should remain with her until her friends returned in spring, or till her brother had "established himself." Rachel herself did not know what to do; and her mind was in a very doubtful condition, full of self-arguments. She did not think Louis would be pleased—that was the dark side. The favourable view was, that she was of use to the invalid, and remaining with her would be "no burden to any one." Rachel pondered, wept, and consulted over it with much sincerity. From the society of these young companions, whom the simple girl loved, and who were so near her own age; from Louis, her lifelong ruler and example; from the kindly fireside, to which she had looked forward so long—it was hard enough to turn to the invalid chambers, the old four-volume novels, and poor pretty old Miss Lucy's "disappointment in love." "And if afterwards I had to sing or give lessons, I should forget all my music there," said Rachel. Mrs Atheling kindly stepped in and decided for her. "It might be a very good thing for you, my dear, if you had no friends," said Mrs Atheling. Rachel did not know whether to be most puzzled or grateful; but to keep a certain conscious solemnity out of her tone—a certain mysterious intimation of something great in the future— was out of the power of Mamma.

Accordingly, they all began their preparations with zeal and energy, the only indifferent member of the party being Agnes, who began to feel herself a good deal alone, and to suspect that she was indeed in the enemy's interest, and not so anxious about the success of Louis as she ought to have been. A few days after Miss Anastasia's visit, the Rector came to find them in all the bustle of preparation. He appeared among them with a certain solemnity, looking haughty and offended, and received Mrs Atheling's intimation of their departure with a grave and punctilious bow. He had evidently known it before, and he looked upon it, quite as evidently, as something done to thwart him—a personal offence to himself.

"Miss Atheling perhaps has literary occupation to call her to town," suggested Mr Rivers, returning to his original ground of displeasure, and trying to get up a little quarrel with Agnes. She did not reply to him, but her mother did, on her behalf.

"Indeed, Mr Rivers, it does not make any difference to Agnes; she can write anywhere," said Mrs Atheling. "I often wonder how she gets on amongst us all; but my husband has been left so long by himself—and now that the trial does not come on till spring, we are all so thankful to get home."

"The trial comes on in spring?—I shall endeavour to be at home," said the Rector, "if I can be of any service. I am myself going to town; I am somewhat unsettled in my plans at present—but my friends whom I esteem most are in London—people of scientific and philosophical pursuits, who cannot afford to be fashionable. Shall I have your permission to call on you when we are all there?"

"I am sure we shall all be very much pleased," said Mrs Atheling, flattered by his tone—"you know what simple people we are, and we do not keep any company; but we shall be very pleased, and honoured too, to see you as we have seen you here."

Agnes was a little annoyed by her mother's speech. She looked up with a flash of indignation, and met, not the eyes of Mrs Atheling, but those of Mr Rivers, who was looking at her. The eyes had a smile in them, but there was perfect gravity upon the face. She was confused by the look, though she did not know why. The words upon her lip were checked—she looked down again, and began to arrange her papers with a rising colour. The Rector's look wandered from her face, because he perceived that he embarrassed her, but went no further than her hands, which were pretty hands enough, yet nothing half so exquisite as those rose-tipped fairy fingers with which Marian folded up her embroidery. The Rector had no eyes at all for Marian; but he watched the arrangement of Agnes's papers with a quite involuntary interest—detected in an instant when she misplaced one, and was very much disposed to offer his own assistance, relenting towards her. What he meant by it—he who was really the heir of Lord Winterbourne, and by no means unaware of his own advantages—Mrs Atheling, looking on with quick-witted maternal observation, could not tell.

Then quite abruptly—after he had watched all Agnes's papers into the pockets of her writing-book—he rose to go away; then he lingered over the ceremony of shaking hands with her, and held hers longer than there was any occasion for. "Some time I hope to resume our argument," said Mr Rivers. He paused till she answered him: "I do not know about argument," said Agnes, looking up with a flash of spirit—"I should be foolish to try it against you. I know only what I trust in—that is not argument—I never meant it so."

He made no reply save by a bow, and went away leaving her rather excited, a little angry, a little moved. Then they began to plague her with questions—What did Mr Rivers mean? There was nothing in the world which Agnes knew less of than what Mr Rivers meant. She tried to explain, in a general way, the conversation she had with him before, but made an extremely lame explanation, which no one was satisfied with, and escaped to her own room in a very nervous condition, quite disturbed out of her self-command. Agnes did not at all know what to make of her anomalous feelings. She was vexed to the heart to feel how much she was interested, while she disapproved so much, and with petulant annoyance exclaimed to herself, that she wanted no more argument if he would but let her alone!

And then came the consideration of Lionel's false hope—the hope which some of these days would be taken from him in a moment. If she could only let him know what she knew, her conscience would be easy. As she thought of this, she remembered how people have been told in fables secrets as important; the idea flashed into her mind with a certain relief— then came the pleasure of creation, the gleam of life among her maze of thoughts; the fancy brightened into shape and graceful fashion—she began unconsciously to hang about it the shining garments of genius—and so she rose and went about her homely business, putting together the little frocks of Bell and Beau, ready to be packed, with the vision growing and brightening before her eyes. Then the definite and immediate purpose of it gave way to a pure native delight in the beautiful thing which began to grow and expand in her thoughts. She went down again, forgetting her vexation. If it did no other good in the world, there was the brightest stream of practical relief and consolation in Agnes Atheling's gift.

CHAPTER XVI
NEW INFLUENCES

Once more the Old Wood Lodge stood solitary under the darkening wintry skies, with no bright faces at its windows, nor gleam of household firelight in the dim little parlour, where Miss Bridget's shadow came back to dwell among the silence, a visionary inhabitant. Once more Hannah sat solitary in her kitchen, lamenting that it was "lonesomer nor ever," and pining for the voices of the children. Hannah would have almost been content to leave her native place and her own people to accompany the family to London; but that was out of the question; and, spite of all Mamma's alarms, Susan had really conducted herself in a very creditable manner under her great responsibility as housekeeper at Bellevue.

The journey home was not a very eventful one. They were met by Papa and Louis on their arrival, and conducted in triumph to their own little house, which did not look so attractive, by any means, as it used to do. Then they settled down without more ado into the family use and wont. With so great a change in all their prospects and intentions—so strange an enlargement of their horizon and extension of their hopes—it was remarkable how little change befell the outward life and customs of the family. Marian, it was true, was "engaged;" but Marian might have been engaged to poor Harry Oswald without any great variation of circumstances; and that was always a possibility lying under everybody's eyes. It did not yet disturb the *habits* of the family; but this new life which they began to enter—this life of separated and individual interest—took no small degree of heart and spirit out of those joint family pleasures and occupations into which Marian constantly brought a reference to Louis, which Agnes passed through with a preoccupied and abstracted mind, and from which Charlie was far away. The stream widened, the sky grew broader, yet every one had his or her separate and peculiar firmament. A maturer, perhaps, and more complete existence was opening upon them; but the first effect was by no means to increase the happiness of the family. They loved each other as well as ever; but they were not so entirely identical. It was a disturbing influence, foreign and unusual; it was not the quiet, assured, undoubting family happiness of the days which were gone.

Then there were other unaccordant elements. Rachel, whom Mrs Atheling insisted upon retaining with them, and who was extremely eager on her own part to find something to do, and terrified to think herself a burden upon her friends; and Louis, who contented himself with his pittance of income, but only did his mere duty at the office, and gave all his thoughts and all his powers to the investigation which engrossed him. Mrs Atheling was very much concerned about Louis. If all this came to nothing, as was quite probable, she asked her husband eagerly what was to become of these young people—what were they to do? For at present, instead of trying to get on, Louis, who had no suspicion of the truth, gave his whole attention to a visionary pursuit, and was content to have the barest enough which he could exist upon. Mr Atheling shook his head, and could not make any satisfactory reply. "There was no disposition to idleness about the boy," Papa said, with approval. "He was working very hard, though he might make nothing by it; and when this state of uncertainty was put an end to, then they should see."

And Marian of late had become actively suspicious and observant. Marian attacked her mother boldly, and without concealment. "Mamma, it is something about Louis that Charlie has gone abroad for!" she said, in an unexpected sally, which took the garrison by surprise.

"My dear, how could you think of such a thing?" cried the prudent Mrs Atheling. "What could Miss Anastasia have to do with Louis? Why, she never so much as saw him, you know. You must, by no means, take foolish fancies into your head. I daresay, after all, he must belong to Lord Winterbourne."

Marian asked no more; but she did not fail to communicate her suspicions to Louis at the earliest opportunity. "I am quite sure," said Marian, not scrupling even to express her convictions in presence of Agnes and Rachel, "that Charlie has gone abroad for something about you."

"Something about me!" Louis was considerably startled; he was even indignant for a moment. He did not relish the idea of having secret enterprises undertaken for him, or to know less about himself than Marian's young brother did. "You must be mistaken," he said, with a momentary haughtiness. "Charlie is a very acute fellow, but I do not see that he is likely to trouble himself about me."

"Oh, but it was Miss Anastasia," said Marian, eagerly.

Then Louis coloured, and drew himself up. His first idea was that Miss Anastasia looked for evidence to prove him the son of Lord Winterbourne; and he resented, with natural vehemence, the interference of the old lady.

"We are come to a miserable pass, indeed," he said, with bitterness, "when people investigate privately to prove this wretched lie against us."

"But you do not understand," cried Rachel. "Oh, Louis, I never told you what Miss Anastasia said. She said you were to take the name of Atheling, because it meant illustrious, and because the exiled princes were named so. Both Marian and Agnes heard her. She is a friend, Louis. Oh, I am sure, if she is inquiring anything, it is all for our good!"

The colour rose still higher upon Louis's cheek. He did not quite comprehend at the moment this strange, sudden side-light which glanced down upon the question which was so important to him. He did not pause to follow, nor see to what it might lead; but it struck him as a clue to something, though he was unable to discover what that something was. Atheling! the youth's imagination flashed back in a moment upon those disinherited descendants of Alfred, the Edgars and Margarets, who, instead of princely titles, bore only that addition to their name. He was as near the truth at that moment as people wandering in profound darkness are often near the light. Another step would have brought him to it; but Louis did not take that step, and was not enlightened. His heart rose, however, with the burning impatience of one who comes within sight of the goal. He started involuntarily with haste and eagerness. He was jealous that even friendly investigations should be the first to find out the mystery. He felt as if he would have a better right to anything which might be awaiting him, if he discovered it himself.

Upon all this tumult of thought and feeling, Agnes looked on, saying nothing—looked on, by no means enjoying her spectatorship and superior knowledge. It was a "situation" which might have pleased Mr Endicott, but it terribly embarrassed Agnes, who found it no pleasure at all to be so much wiser than her neighbours. She dared not confide the secret to Louis any more than she could to the Rector; and she would have been extremely unhappy between them, but for the relief and comfort of that fable, which was quickly growing into shape and form. It had passed out of her controlling hands already, and began to exercise over her the sway which a real created thing always exercises over the mind even of its author: it had ceased to be the direct personal affair she had intended to make it; it told its story, but after a more delicate process, and Agnes expended all her graceful fancy upon its perfection. She thought now that Louis might find it out as well as the Rector. It was an eloquent appeal, heart-warm and touching to them both.

CHAPTER XVII
RACHEL'S DOUBTS

After Louis, the most urgent business in the house of the Athelings was that of Rachel, who was so pertinaciously anxious to be employed, that her friends found it very difficult to evade her constant entreaties. Rachel's education—or rather Rachel's want of education—had been very different from that of Marian and Agnes. She had no traditions of respectability to deter her from anything she could do; and she had been accustomed to sing to the guests at Winterbourne, and concluded that it would make very little difference to her, whether her performance was in a public concert-room or a private assembly. "No one would care at all for me; no one would ever think of me or look at me," said Rachel. "If I sang well, that would be all that any one thought of; and we need not tell Louis—and I would not mind myself—and no one would ever know."

"But I have great objections to it, my dear," said Mrs Atheling, with some solemnity. "I should rather a hundred times take in work myself, or do anything with my own hands, than let my girls do this. It is not respectable for a young girl. A public appearance! I should be grieved and ashamed beyond anything. I should indeed, my dear."

"I am very sorry, Mrs Atheling," said Rachel, wistfully; "but it is not anything wrong."

"Not wrong—but not at all respectable," said Mrs Atheling, "and unfeminine, and very dangerous indeed, and a discreditable position for a young girl."

Rachel blushed, and was very much disconcerted, but still did not give up the point. "I thought it so when they tried to force me," she said in a low tone; "but now, no one need know; and people, perhaps, might have me at their houses; ladies sing in company. You would not mind me doing that, Mrs Atheling? Or I could give lessons. Perhaps you think it is all vanity; but indeed they used to think me a very good singer, long ago. Oh, Agnes, do you remember that old gentleman at the Willow? that very old gentleman who used to talk to you? I think he could help me if you would only speak to him."

"Mr Agar? I think he could," said Agnes; "but, Rachel, mamma says you must not think of it. Marian does not do anything, and why should you?"

"I am no one's daughter," said Rachel, sadly. "You are all very kind; but Louis has only a very little money; and I will not—indeed I will not—be a burden upon you."

"Rachel, my dear," said Mrs Atheling, "do not speak so foolishly; but I will tell you what we can do. Agnes shall write down all about it to Miss Anastasia, and ask her advice, and whether she consents to it; and if she consents, I will not object any more. I promise I shall not stand in the way at all, if Miss Anastasia decides for you."

Rachel looked up with a little wonder. "But Miss Anastasia has nothing to do with us," said the astonished girl. "I would rather obey you than Miss Rivers, a great deal. Why should we consult *her*?"

"My dear," said Mrs Atheling, with importance, "you must not ask any questions at present. *I have my reasons.* Miss Anastasia takes a great interest in you, and I have a very good reason for what I say."

This made an end of the argument; but Rachel was extremely puzzled, and could not understand it. She was not very quick-witted, this gentle little girl; she began to have a certain awe of Miss Anastasia, and to suppose that it must be her superior wisdom which made every one ask her opinion. Rachel could not conclude upon any other reason, and accordingly awaited with a little solemnity the decision of Miss Rivers. They were in a singular harmony, all these young people; not one of them but had some great question hanging in the balance, which they themselves were not sufficient to conclude upon—something that might change and colour the whole course of their lives.

Another event occurring just at this time, made Rachel for a time the heroine of the family. Charlie wrote home with great regularity, like a good son as he was. His letters were very short, and not at all explanatory; but they satisfied his mother that he had not taken a fever, nor fallen into the hands of robbers, and that was so far well. In one of these epistles, however, the young gentleman extended his brief report a little, to describe to them a family with which he had formed acquaintance. There were a lot of girls, Charlie said; and one of them, called Giulia Remori, was strangely like "Miss Rachel;" "not exactly like," wrote Charlie,—"not like Agnes and Marian" (who, by the way, had only a very vague resemblance to each other). "You would not suppose them to be sisters; but I always think of Miss Rachel when I see this Signora Giulia. They say, too, she has a great genius for music, and I heard her sing once myself, like——; well, I cannot say what it was like. The most glorious music, I believe, under the skies."

"Mamma, that cannot be Charlie!" said the girls simultaneously; but it was Charlie, without any dispute, and Marian clapped her hands in triumph, and exclaimed that he must be in love; and there stood Rachel, very much interested, wistful, and smiling. The tender-hearted girl had the greatest propensity to make friendships. She received the idea of this foreign Giulia into her heart in a moment, and ran forth eagerly at the time of Louis's usual evening visit to meet him at the gate, and tell him this little bit of romance. It moved Louis a great deal more deeply than it moved Rachel. This time his eye flashed to the truth like lightning. He began to give serious thought to what Marian had said of Charlie's object, and of Miss Anastasia. "Hush, Rachel," he said, with sudden gravity. "Hush, I see it; this is some one belonging to our mother."

"Our mother!" The two orphans stood together at the little gate, silenced by the name. They had never speculated much upon this parent. It was one of the miseries of their cruel position, that the very idea of a dead mother, which is to most minds the most saintlike and holy imagination under heaven, brought to them their bitterest pang of disgrace and humiliation. Yet now Louis stood silent, pondering it with the deepest eagerness. A burning impatience possessed the young man; a violent colour rose over his face. He could not tolerate the idea of an unconcerned inquirer into matters so instantly momentous to himself. He was not at all amiable in his impulses; his immediate and wild fancy was to rush away, on foot and penniless, as he was; to turn off Charlie summarily from his mission, if he had one; and without a clue, or a guide, or a morsel of information which pointed in that direction, by sheer force of energy and desperation to find it out himself. It was misery to go in quietly to the quiet house, even to the presence of Marian, with such a fancy burning in his mind. He left Rachel abruptly, without a word of explanation, and went off to make inquiries about travelling. It was perfectly vain, but it was some satisfaction to the fever of his mind. Louis's defection made Marian very angry; when he came next day they had their first quarrel, and parted in great distraction and misery, mutually convinced of the treachery and wretchedness of this world; but made it up again very shortly after, to the satisfaction of every one concerned. With these things happening day by day, with their impatient and fiery Orlando, always in some degree inflaming the house, it is not necessary to say how wonderful a revolution had been wrought upon the quiet habitudes of this little house in Bellevue.

CHAPTER XVIII
AGNES

Yet the household felt, in spite of itself, a difference by no means agreeable between the Old Wood Lodge and Bellevue. The dull brick wall of Laurel House was not nearly so pleasant to look upon as that great amphitheatre with its maze of wan waters and willow-trees, where the sunshine flashed among the spires of Oxford; neither was Miss Willsie, kind and amusing as she was, at all a good substitute for Miss Anastasia. They had Louis, it was true, but Louis was in love, and belonged to Marian; and no one within their range was at all to be compared to the Rector. Accustomed to have their interest fixed, after their own cottage, upon the Old Wood House and Winterbourne Hall, they were a little dismayed, in spite of themselves, to see the meagreness and small dimensions even of Killiecrankie Lodge. It was a different world altogether—and they did not know at the first glance how to make the two compatible. The little house in the country, now that they had left it, grew more and more agreeable by comparison. Mrs Atheling forgot that she had thought it damp, and all of them, Mamma herself among the rest, began to think of their return in spring.

And as the winter went on, Agnes made progress with her fable. She did not write it carefully, but she did write it with fervour, and the haste of a mind concerned and in earnest. The story had altered considerably since she first thought of it. There was in it a real heir whom nobody knew, and a supposed heir, who was the true hero of the book. The real heir had a love-story, and the prettiest *fiancée* in the world; but about her hero Agnes was timid, presenting a grand vague outline of him, and describing him in sublime general terms; for she was not at all an experienced young lady, though she was an author, but herself regarded her hero with a certain awe and respect and imperfect understanding, as young men and young women of poetic conditions are wont to regard each other. From this cause it resulted that you were not very clear about the Sir Charles Grandison of the young novelist. Her pretty heroine was as clear as a sunbeam; and even the Louis of her story was definable, and might be recognised; but the other lay half visible, sometimes shining out in a sudden gleam of somewhat tremulous light, but for the most part enveloped in shadow: everybody else in the tale spoke of him, thought of him, and were marvellously influenced by him; but his real appearances were by no means equal to the importance he had acquired.

The sole plot of the story was connected with the means by which the unsuspected heir came to a knowledge of his rights, and gained his true place; and there was something considerably exciting to Agnes in her present exercise of the privilege of fiction, and the steps she took to make the title of her imaginary Louis clear. She used to pause, and wonder in the midst of it, whether such chances as these would befall the true Louis, and how far the means of her invention would resemble the real means. It was a very odd occupation, and interested her strangely. It was not very much of a story, neither was it written with that full perfection of style which comes by experience and the progress of years; but it had something in its faulty grace, and earnestness, and simplicity, which was perhaps more attractive than the matured perfectness of a style which had been carefully formed, and "left nothing to desire." It was sparkling with youth, and it was warm from the heart. It went into no greater bulk than one small volume, which Mr Burlington put into glowing red cloth, embellished with two engravings, and ornamented with plenty of gilding. It came out, a wintry Christmas flower, making no such excitement in the house as *Hope Hazlewood* had done; and Agnes had the satisfaction of handing over to Papa, to lock up in his desk in the office, a delightfully crisp, crackling, newly-issued fifty-pound note.

And Christmas had just given way to the New Year when the Rector made his appearance at Bellevue. He was still more eager, animated, and hopeful than he had been when they saw him last. His extreme high-church clerical costume was entirely abandoned; he still wore black, but it was not very professional, and he appeared in these unknown parts with books in his hands and smiles on his face. When he came into the little parlour, he did not seem at all to notice its limited dimensions, but greeted them all with an effusion of pleasure and kindness, which greatly touched the heart of Agnes, and moved her mother, in her extreme gratification and pride, to something very like tears. Mr Rivers inquired at once for Louis, with great gravity and interest, but shook his head when he heard what his present occupation was.

"This will not do; will he come and see me, or shall I wait upon him?" said the Rector with a subdued smile, as he remembered the youthful haughtiness of Louis. "I should be glad to speak to him about his prospects—here is my card—will you kindly ask him to dine with me to-night, alone? He is a young man of great powers; something better may surely be found for him than this lawyer's office."

Mrs Atheling was a little piqued in spite of herself. "My son, when he is at home, is there," said the good mother; and her visitor did not fail to see the significance of the tone.

"He is not at home now—where is he?" said the Rector.

There was a moment's hesitation. Agnes turned to look at him, her colour rising violently, and Mrs Atheling faltered in her reply.

"He has gone abroad to —— to make some inquiries," said Mrs Atheling; "though he is so very young, people have great confidence in him; and—and it may turn out very important indeed, what he has gone about."

Once more Agnes cast a troubled glance upon the Rector—he heard of it with such perfect unconcern—this inquiry which in a moment might strike his ambition to the dust.

He ceased at once speaking on this subject, which did not interest him. He said, turning to her, that he had brought some books about which he wanted Miss Atheling's opinion. Agnes shrank back immediately in natural diffidence, but revived again, before she was aware, in all her old impulse of opposition. "If it is wrong to write books, is it right to form opinions upon them?" said Agnes. Mr Rivers imperceptibly grew a little loftier and statelier as she spoke.

"I think I have explained my sentiments on that point," said the Rector; "there is no one whose appreciation I should set so high a value on as that of an intelligent woman."

It was Agnes's turn to blush and say nothing, as she met his eye. When Mr Rivers said "an intelligent woman," he meant, though the expression was not romantic, his own ideal; and there lay his books upon the table, evidences of his choice of a critic. She began to busy herself with them, looking quite vacantly at the title-pages; wondering if there was anything besides books, and controversies, and opinions, to be found in the Rector's heart.

When Mrs Atheling, in her natural pride and satisfaction, bethought her of that pretty little book with its two illustrations, and its cover in crimson and gold, she brought a copy to the table immediately. "My dear, perhaps Mr Rivers might like to look at this?" said Mrs Atheling. "It has only been a week published, but people speak very well of it already. It is a very pretty story. I think you would like it—Agnes, my love, write Mr Rivers' name."

"No, no, mamma!" cried Agnes hurriedly; she put away the red book from her, and went away from the table in haste and agitation. Very true, it was written almost for him—but she was dismayed at the idea of being called to write in it Lionel Rivers' name.

He took up the book, however, and looked at it in the gravest silence. *The Heir;*—he read the title aloud, and it seemed to strike him; then without another word he put the little volume safely in his pocket, repeated his message to Louis, and a few minutes afterwards, somewhat grave and abstracted, took his leave of them, and hastened away.

CHAPTER XIX
LIONEL

The Rector became a very frequent visitor during the few following weeks at Bellevue. Louis had gone to see him, as he desired, and Mr Rivers anxiously endeavoured to persuade the youth to suffer himself to be "assisted." Louis as strenuously resisted every proposal of the kind; he was toiling on in pursuit of himself, through his memoir of Lord Winterbourne—still eager, and full of expectation—still proud, and refusing to be indebted to any one. The Rector argued with him like an elder brother. "Let us grant that you are successful," said Mr Rivers; "let us suppose that you make an unquestionable discovery, what position are you in to pursue it? Your sister, even—recollect your sister—you cannot provide for her."

His sister was Louis's grand difficulty; he bit his lip, and the fiery glow of shame came to his face. "I cannot provide for her, it is true. I am bitterly ashamed of it; but, at least, she is among friends."

"You do me small credit," said the Rector; "but I will not ask, on any terms, for a friendship which is refused to me. You are not even in the way of advancement; and to lose your time after this fashion is madness. Let me see you articled to these people whom you are with now; that is, at least, a chance, though not a great one. If I can accomplish it, will you consent to this?"

Louis paused a little, grateful in his heart, though his tongue was slow to utter his sentiments. "You are trying to do me a great service," said the young man; "you think me a churl, and ungrateful, but you endeavour to benefit me against my will—is it not true? I am just in such a position that no miracle in the world would seem wonderful to me; it is possible, in the chances of the future, that we two may be set up against each other. I cannot accept this service from you—from you, or from any other. I must wait."

The Rector turned away almost with impatience. "Do you suppose you can spend your life in this fashion—your life?" he exclaimed, with some heat.

"My life!" said Louis. He was a little startled with this conclusion. "I thank you," he added abruptly, "for your help, for your advice, for your reproof—I thank you heartily, but I have no more to say."

That was how the conversation ended. Lionel, grieved for the folly of the boy, smiling to himself at Louis's strange delusion that he, who was the very beau-ideal of the race of Rivers, belonged to another house, went to his rest, with a mind disturbed, full of difficulties, and of ambition, working out one solemn problem, and touched with tender dreams; yet always remembering, with a pleasure which he could not restrain, the great change in his position, and that he was now, not merely the Rector, but the heir of Winterbourne. Louis, on his part, went home to his dark little lodging, with the swell and tumult of excitement in his mind, and could not sleep. He seemed to be dizzied with the rushing shadows of a crowd of coming events. He was not well; his abstinence, his studiousness, his change of place and life, had weakened his young frame; these rushing wings seemed to tingle in his ears, and his temples throbbed as if they kept time. He rose in the middle of the night, in the deep wintry silence and moonlight, to open his window, and feel the cold air upon his brow. There he saw the moonbeams falling softly, not on any imposing scene, but on the humble roof underneath whose shelter sweet voices and young hearts, devout and guileless, prayed for him every night; the thought calmed him into sudden humility and quietness; and, in his poverty, and hope, and youth, he returned to his humble bed, and slept. Lionel was waking too; but he did not know of any one who prayed for *him* in all this cold-hearted world.

But the Rector became a very frequent visitor in Bellevue. He had read the little book—read it with a kind of startled consciousness, the first time, that it looked like a true story, and seemed somehow familiar to himself. But by-and-by he began to keep it by him, and, not for the sake of the story, to take it up idly when he was doing nothing else, and refer to it as a kind of companion. It was not, in any degree whatever, an intellectual display; he by no means felt himself pitted against the author of it, or entering into any kind of rivalship with her. The stream sparkled and flashed to the sunshine as it ran; but it flowed with a sweet spontaneous readiness, and bore no trace of artificial force and effort. It wanted a great many of the qualities which critics praise. There was no great visible strain of power, no forcible evidence of difficulties overcome. The reader knew very well that *he* could not have done this, nor anything like it, yet his intellectual pride was not roused. It was genius solacing itself with its own romaunt, singing by the way; it was not talent getting up an exhibition for the astonishment, or the enlightenment, or the instruction of others. Agnes defeated her own purpose by the very means she had taken to procure it. The Rector forgot all about the story, thinking of the writer of it; he became indifferent to what she had to tell, but dwelt and lingered—not like a critic—like something very different—upon the cadence of her voice.

To tell the truth, between his visits to Bellevue, and his musings thereafter—his study of this little fable of Agnes's, and his vague mental excursions into the future, Lionel Rivers, had he yielded to the fascination, would have found very near enough to do. But he was manful enough to resist this trance of fairyland. He was beginning to be "in love;" nobody could dispute it; it was visible enough to wake the most entire sympathy in the breasts of Marian and Rachel, and to make for the mother of the family wakeful nights, and a most uneasy pillow; but he was far from being at ease or in peace. His friends in London were of a class as different as possible from these humble people who were rapidly growing nearer than friends. They were all men of great intelligence, of great powers, scholars, philosophers, authorities—men who belonged, and professed to belong, to the ruling class of intellect, prophets and apostles of a new generation. They were not much given to believing anything, though some among them had a weakness for mesmerism or spiritual manifestations. They investigated all beliefs and faculties of believing, and received all marvellous stories, from the Catholic legends of the saints to the miracles of the New Testament, on one general ground of indulgence, charitable and tender, as mythical stories which meant something in their day. Most of them wrote an admirable style— most of them occasionally said very profound things which nobody could understand; all of them were scholars and gentlemen, as blameless in their lives as they were superior in their powers; and all of them lived upon a kind of intellectual platform, philosophical demigods, sufficient for themselves, and looking down with a good deal of curiosity, a little contempt, and a little pity, upon the crowds who thronged below of common men.

These were the people to whom Lionel Rivers, in the first flush of his emancipation, had hastened from his high-churchism, and his country pulpit—some of them had been his companions at College—some had inspired him by their books, or pleased him by their eloquence. They were a brotherhood of men of great cultivation—his equals, and sometimes his superiors. He had yearned for their society when he was quite removed from it; but he was of a perverse and unconforming mind. What did he do now?

He took the strange fancy suddenly, and telling no man, of wandering through those frightful regions of crime and darkness, which we hide behind our great London streets. He went about through the miserable thoroughfares, looking at the miserable creatures there. What was the benefit to them of these polluted lives of theirs? They had their enjoyments, people said—their enjoyments! Their sorrows, like the sorrows of all humanity, were worthy human tears, consolation, and sympathy,—their hardships and endurances were things to move the universal heart; but their enjoyments—Heaven save us!—the pleasures of St Giles's, the delights and amusements of those squalid groups at the street corners! If they were to have nothing more than that, what a frightful fate was theirs!

And there came upon the spectator, as he went among them in silence, a sudden eagerness to try that talisman which Agnes Atheling had bidden him use. It was vain to try philosophy there, where no one knew what it meant— vain to offer the rites of the Church to those who were fatally beyond its pale. Was it possible, after all, that the one word in the world, which could stir something human—something of heaven—in these degraded breasts, was that one sole unrivalled *Name*?

He could not withdraw himself from the wretched scene before him. He went on from street to street with something of the consciousness of a man who carries a hidden remedy through a plague-stricken city, but hides his knowledge in his own mind, and does not apply it. A strange sense of guilt—a strange oppression by reason of this grand secret—an overpowering passionate impulse to try the solemn experiment, and withal a fascinated watchfulness which kept him silent—possessed the mind of the young man.

He walked about the streets like a man doing penance; then he began to notice other passengers not so idle as himself. There were people here who were trying to break into the mass of misery, and make a footing for purity and light among it. They were not like his people;—sometimes they were poor city missionaries, men of very bad taste, not perfect in their grammar, and with no great amount of discretion. Even the people of higher class were very limited people often to the perception of Mr Rivers; but they were at work, while the demigods slept upon their platform. It would be very hard to make philosophers of the wretched population here. Philosophy did not break its heart over the impossibility, but calmly left the untasteful city missionaries, the clergymen, High Church and Low Church, who happened to be in earnest, and some few dissenting ministers of the neighbourhood, labouring upon a forlorn hope to make them *men*.

All this moved in the young man's heart as he pursued his way among these squalid streets. Every one of these little stirrings in this frightful pool of stagnant life was made in the name of Him whom Lionel Rivers once named with cold irreverence, and whom Agnes Atheling, with a tender awe and appropriation, called "Our Lord." This was the problem he was busy with while he remained in London. It was not one much discussed, either in libraries or drawing-rooms, among his friends; he discussed it by himself as he wandered through St Giles's—silent—watching—with the great Name which he himself did not know, but began to cling to as a talisman, burning at his heart.

CHAPTER XX
AN ARRIVAL

While the Athelings at home were going on quietly, but with anxiety and disturbance of mind in this way, they were startled one afternoon by a sudden din and tumult out of doors, nearly as great as that which, not much short of a year ago, had announced the first call of Mrs Edgerley. It was not, however, a magnificent equipage like that of the fashionable patroness of literature which drew up at the door now. It was an antique job carriage, not a very great deal better to look at than that venerable fly of Islington, which was still regarded with respect by Agnes and Marian. In this vehicle there were two horses, tall brown bony old hacks, worthy the equipage they drew—an old coachman in a very ancient livery, and an active youth, fresh, rural, and ruddy, who sprang down from the creaking coach-box to assault, but in a moderate country fashion, the door of the Athelings. Rachel, who was peeping from the window, uttered an exclamation of surprise—"Oh, Agnes, look! it is Miss Anastasia's man."

It was so beyond dispute, and Miss Anastasia herself immediately descended from the creaking vehicle, swinging heavily upon its antiquated springs; she had a large cloak over her brown pelisse, and a great muff of rich sables, big enough to have covered from head to foot, like a case, either little Bell or little Beau. She was so entirely like herself in spite of those additions to her characteristic costume, and withal so unlike other people, that they could have supposed she had driven here direct from the Priory, had that been possible, without any commonplace intervention of railway or locomotive by the way. As the girls came to the door to meet her, she took the face—first of Agnes, then of Marian, and lastly of Rachel, who was a good deal dismayed by the honour—between her hands, thrusting the big muff, like a prodigious bracelet, up upon her arm the while, and kissed them with a cordial heartiness. Then she went into the little parlour to Mrs Atheling, who in the mean time had been gathering together the scattered pieces of work, and laying them, after an orderly fashion, in her basket. Then Papa's easy-chair was wheeled to the fire for the old lady, and Marian stooped to find a footstool for her, and Agnes helped to loose the big cloak from her shoulders. Miss Anastasia's heart was touched by the attentions of the young people. She laid her large hand caressingly on Marian's head, and patted the cheek of Agnes. "Good children—eh? I missed them," she said, turning to Mamma, and Mamma brightened with pleasure and pride as she whispered something to Agnes about the fire in the best room. Then, when she had held a little conversation with the girls, Miss Rivers began to look uneasy. She glanced at Mrs Atheling with a clear intention of making some telegraphic communication; she glanced at the girls and at the door, and back again at Mamma, with a look full of meaning. Mrs Atheling was not generally so dull of comprehension, but she was so full of the idea that Miss Anastasia's real visit was to the girls, and so proud of the attraction which even this dignified old lady could not resist, that she could not at all consent to believe that Miss Rivers desired to be left alone with herself.

"There's a hamper from the Priory," said Miss Anastasia at last, abruptly; "among other country things there's some flowers in it, children—make haste all of you and get it unpacked, and tell me what you think of my camellias! Make haste, girls!"

It was a most moving argument; but it distracted Mrs Atheling's attention almost as much as that of her daughters, for the hamper doubtless contained something else than flowers. Mamma, however, remained decorously with her guest, despite the risk of breakage to the precious country eggs; and the girls, partly deceived, partly suspecting their visitor's motive, obeyed her injunction, and hastened away. Then Miss Rivers caught Mrs Atheling by the sleeve, and drew her close towards her. "Have you heard from your boy?" said Miss Anastasia.

"No," said Mrs Atheling with a sudden momentary alarm, "not for a week—has anything happened to Charlie?"

"Nonsense—what could happen to him?" cried the old lady, with a little impatience, "here is a note I had this morning—read it—he is coming home."

Mrs Atheling took the letter with great eagerness. It was a very brief one:—

Madam,—I have come to it at last—suddenly. I have only time to tell you so. I shall leave to-day with an important witness. I have not even had leisure to write to my mother; but will push on to the Priory whenever I have bestowed my witness safely in Bellevue. In great haste.—Your obedient servant,

C. Atheling.

Charlie's mother trembled all over with agitation and joy. She had to grasp by the mantel-shelf to keep herself quite steady. She exclaimed, "My own boy!" half-crying and wholly exultant, and would have liked to have hurried out forthwith upon the road and met him half-way, had that been possible. She kept the letter in her hand looking at it, and quite forgetting that it belonged to Miss Anastasia. He had justified the trust put in him—he had crowned himself with honour—he was coming home! Not much wonder that the good mother was weeping-ripe, and could have sobbed aloud for very joy.

"Ay," said Miss Anastasia, with something like a sigh, "you're a rich woman. I have not rested since this came to me, nor can I rest till I hear all your boy has to say."

At this moment Mrs Atheling started with a little alarm, catching from the window a glimpse of the coach, with its two horses and its antiquated coachman, slowly turning round and driving away. Miss Anastasia followed her glance with a subdued smile.

"Do you mean then to—to stay in London, Miss Rivers?" asked Mrs Atheling.

"Tut! the boy will be home directly—to-night," said Miss Anastasia; "I meant to wait here until he came."

Mrs Atheling started again in great and evident perturbation. You could perceive that she repeated "to wait *here!*" within herself with a great many points of admiration; but she was too well-bred to express her dismay. She cast, however, an embarrassed look round her, said she should be very proud, and Miss Rivers would do them honour, but she was afraid the accommodation was not equal—and here Mrs Atheling paused much distressed.

"I have been calculating all the way up when he can be here," interrupted Miss Anastasia. "I should say about twelve o'clock to-night. Agnes, when she comes back again, shall revise it for me. Never mind accommodation. Give him an hour's grace—say he comes at one o'clock—then a couple of hours later—by that time it will be three in the morning. Then I am sure one of the girls will not grudge me her bed till six. We'll get on very well; and when Will Atheling comes home, if you have anything to say to him, I can easily step out of the way. Well, am I an intruder? If I am not, don't say anything more about it. I cannot rest till I see the boy."

When the news became diffused through the house that Charlie was coming home to-night, and that Miss Anastasia was to wait for him, a very great stir and bustle immediately ensued. The best room was hastily put in order, and Mrs Atheling's own bedchamber immediately revised and beautified for the reception of Miss Anastasia. It was with a little difficulty, however, that the old lady was persuaded to leave the family parlour for the best room. She resisted energetically all unusual attentions, and did not hesitate to declare, even in the presence of Rachel, that her object was to see Charlie, and that for his arrival she was content to wait all night. A great anxiety immediately took possession of the household. They too were ready and eager to wait all night; and even Susan became vaguely impressed with a solemn sense of some great approaching event. Charlie was not to be alone either. The excitement rose to a quite overpowering pitch—who was coming with him? What news did he bring? These questions prolonged to the most insufferable tediousness the long slow darksome hours of the March night.

CHAPTER XXI
CHARLIE'S RETURN

The girls could not be persuaded to go to rest, let Mamma say what she would. Rachel, the only one who had no pretence, nor could find any excuse for sitting up, was the only one who showed the least sign of obedience; *she* went up-stairs with a meek unwillingness, lingered as long as she could before lying down, and when she extinguished her light at last, lay very broad awake looking into the midnight darkness, and listening anxiously to every sound below. Marian, in the parlour on a footstool, sat leaning both her arms on her mother's knee, and her head upon her arms, and in that position had various little sleeps, and half-a-dozen times in half-a-dozen dreams welcomed Charlie home. Agnes kept Miss Anastasia company in the best room, and Papa, who was not used to late hours, went between the two rooms with very wide open eyes, very anxious for his son's return. Into the midnight darkness and solemnity of Bellevue, the windows of Number Ten blazed with a cheerful light; the fires were studiously kept up, the hearths swept, everything looking its brightest for Charlie; and a pair of splendid capons, part produce of Miss Anastasia's hamper, were slowly cooking themselves into perfection, under the sleepy superintendence of Susan, before the great kitchen-fire—for even Susan would not go to bed.

Miss Anastasia sat very upright in an easy-chair, scorning so much as a suspicion of drowsiness. She did not talk very much; she was thinking over a hundred forgotten things, and tracing back step by step the story of the past. The old lady almost felt as if her father himself was coming from his foreign grave to bear witness to the truth. Her heart was stirred as she sat gazing into the ruddy firelight, hearing not a sound except now and then the ashes falling softly on the hearth, or the softer breath of Agnes by her side. As she sat in this unfamiliar little room, her mind flew back over half her life. She thought of her father as she had seen him last; she thought of the dreary blank of her own youthful desolation, a widowhood almost deeper than the widowhood of a wife—how she did not heed even the solemn pathos of her father's farewell—could not rouse herself from her lethargy even to be moved by the last parting from that last and closest friend, and desired nothing but to be left in her dreary self-seclusion obstinately mourning her dead—her murdered bridegroom! The old lady's eyes glittered, tearless, looking into the gleaming shadowy depths of the little mirror over the mantelpiece. It was scarcely in human nature to look back upon that dreadful tragedy, to anticipate the arrival to-night of the witnesses of another deadly wrong, and not to be stirred with a solemn and overwhelming indignation like that of an avenger of blood. Miss Anastasia started suddenly from her reverie, as she caught a long-drawn anxious sigh from her young companion; she drew her shawl close round her with a shudder. "God forgive me!" cried the vehement old lady; "did you ever have an enemy, child?"

In this house it was a very easy question. "No," said Agnes, looking at her wistfully.

"Nor I, perhaps, when I was your age." Miss Anastasia made a long pause. It was a long time ago, and she scarcely could recollect anything of her youth now, except that agony with which it ended. Then in the silence there seemed to be a noise in the street, which roused all the watchers. Mr Atheling went to the door to look out. It was very cold, clear, and calm, the air so sharp with frost, and so still with sleep, that it carried every passing sound far more distinctly than usual. Into this hushed and anxious house, through the open door came ringing the chorus of a street ballad, strangely familiar and out of unison with the excited feelings of the auditors, and the loud, noisy, echoing footsteps of some late merry-makers. They were all singularly disturbed by these uncongenial sounds; they raised a certain vague terror in the breasts of the father and mother, and a doubtful uneasiness among the other watchers. Under that veil of night, and silence, and distance, who could tell what their dearest and most trusted was doing? The old people could have told each other tales, like Jessica, of "such a night;" and the breathless silence, and the jar and discord of those rude voices, stirred memories and presentiments of pain even in the younger hearts.

It was now the middle of the night, two or three hours later than Miss Anastasia had anticipated, and the old lady rose from her chair, shook off her thoughtful mood, and began to walk about the room, and to criticise it briskly to Agnes. Then by way of diversifying her vigil, she made an incursion into the other parlour, where Papa was nursing the fire, and Mamma sitting very still, not to disturb Marian, who slept with her beautiful head upon her mother's knee. The old lady was suddenly overcome by the sight of that fair figure, with its folded arms and bowed head, and long beautiful locks falling down on Mrs Atheling's dark gown, like a stream of sunshine. She laid her hand very tenderly upon the sleeper's head. "She does not know," said Miss Anastasia—"she would not believe what a fairy fortune is coming to her, the sleeping beauty—God bless them all!"

The words had scarcely left her lips, the tears were still shining in her eyes, when Marian started up, called out of her dream by a sound which none of them besides had been quick enough to hear. "There! there! I hear him," cried Marian, shaking back her loose curls; and they all heard the far-off rapid rumble of a vehicle, gradually invading all the echoes of this quietness. It came along steadily—nearer—nearer—waking every one to the most overpowering excitement. Miss Anastasia marched through the little parlour, with an echoing step, throwing her tall shadow on the blind, clasping her fingers tight. Mr Atheling rushed to the door; Marian ran to the kitchen to wake up Susan, and see that the tray was ready for Charlie's refreshment; Mamma stirred the fire, and made it blaze; Agnes drew the blind aside, and looked out into the darkness from the window. Yes, there could be no mistake; on came the rumbling wheels, closer and closer. Then the cab became absolutely visible, opposite the door—some one leapt out— was it Charlie?—but he had to wait, to help some one else, very slow and uncertain, out of the vehicle. They all crowded to the door, the mother and sisters for the moment half forgetting Miss Anastasia; and there stood a most indisputable Charlie, very near six feet high, with a travelling-cap and a rough overcoat, bringing home the most extraordinary guest imaginable to his amazed parental home.

It was a woman, enveloped from head to foot in a great cloak, but unbonneted, and with an amazing head-dress; and after her stumbled forth a boy, of precisely the same genus and appearance as the Italian boys with hurdy-gurdies and with images, familiar enough in Bellevue. Charlie hurried forward, paying the greatest possible attention to his charge, who was somewhat peevish. He scarcely left her hand when he plunged among all those anxious people at the door. "All safe—all well, mother; how did you know I was coming?—how d'ye do, papa? Let her in, let her in, girls!— she's tired to death, and doesn't know a word of English. Let's have her disposed of first of all—she's worth her weight in gold—— Miss Rivers!"

The young man fell back in extreme amazement. "Who is she, young Atheling?" cried Miss Anastasia, towering high in the background over everybody's head.

Charlie took off his cap with a visible improvement of "manners." "The nurse that brought them home," he answered, in the concisest and most satisfactory fashion; and, grasping the hand of every one as he passed, with real pleasure glowing on his bronzed face, Charlie steered his charge in—seeing there was light in it—to the best room. Arrived there, he fairly turned his back to the wall, and harangued his anxious audience.

"It's all right," said Charlie; "she tells her story as clearly as possible when she's not out of humour, and the doctor's on his way. I've made sure of everything of importance; and now, mother, if you can manage it, and Miss Rivers does not object, let us have something to eat, and get her off to bed, and then you shall hear all the rest."

Marian went off instantly to call Susan, and all the way Marian repeated under her breath, "All the rest! all the rest of what? Oh, Louis! but I'll find out what they mean."

CHAPTER XXII
CHARLIE'S REPORT

It was far from an easy achievement to get her safely conveyed up the stairs. She turned round and delivered addresses to them in most lively and oratorical Italian, eloquent on the subject of her sufferings by the way; she was disposed to be out of temper when no one answered her but Charlie, and fairly wound up, and stimulated with Miss Anastasia's capon and Mrs Atheling's wine, was not half so much disposed to be sent off to bed as her entertainers were to send her. These entertainers were in the oddest state of amaze and excitement possible. It was beginning to draw near the wintry morning of another day, and this strange figure in the strange dress, which did not look half so pretty in its actual reality, and upon this hard-featured peasant woman, as it did in pictures and romance—the voluble foreign tongue of which they did not know a word—the emphatic gestures; the change in the appearance of Charlie, and the entire suddenness of the whole scene, confused the minds of the lookers-on. Then a pale face in a white cap, a little shrinking white-robed figure, trembling and anxious, was perceptible to Mrs Atheling at the top of the stair, looking down upon it with terror. So Mamma peremptorily sent Charlie back beside Miss Anastasia, and resumed into her own hands the management of affairs. Under her guidance the woman and the boy were comfortably disposed of, no one being able to speak a word to them, in the room which had been Charlie's. Rachel was comforted and sent back to bed, and then Mrs Atheling turned suddenly upon her own girls. "My dears," said Mamma, "you are not wanted down stairs. I don't suppose Papa and I are wanted either; Miss Anastasia must talk over her business with Charlie—it is not *our* business you know, Marian, my darling; go to sleep."

"Go to sleep!—people cannot go to sleep just when they choose at five o'clock in the morning, mamma!" cried the aggrieved and indignant Marian; but Agnes, though quite as curious as her sister, was wise enough to lend her assistance in the cause of subordination. Marian was under very strong temptation. She thought she could *almost* like to steal down in the dark and listen; but honour, we are glad to say, prevailed over curiosity, and sleep over both. When her pretty young head touched the pillow, there was no eavesdropping possible to Marian; and in the entirest privacy and silence, after all this tumult, in the presence of Mamma and Mr Atheling, and addressing himself to Miss Anastasia, Charlie told his tale. He took out his pocket-book from his pocket—the same old-fashioned big pocket-book which he had carried away with him, and gave his evidences one by one into Miss Anastasia's hands as he spoke.

But the old lady's fingers trembled: she had restrained herself as well as she could, feeling it only just that he should be welcomed by his own, and even half diverted out of her anxiety by the excited Tyrolese; but now her restrained feelings rushed back upon her heart. The papers rustled in her hand; she did not hear him as he began, in order, and deliberately, his report. "Information! I cannot receive information, I am too far gone for that," cried the old lady, with a hysterical break in her voice. "Give me no facts, Charlie, Charlie!—I am not able to put them together—tell me once in a word—is it true?"

"It is true," said Charlie, eagerly—"not only true, but proved—certain, so clear that nobody can deny it. Listen, Miss Rivers, I could be content to go by myself with these evidences in my hand, before any court in England, against the ablest pleader that ever held a brief. Don't mind the proofs to-night; trust my assurance, as you trusted me. It is true to the letter, to the word, everything that you supposed. Giulietta was his wife. Louis is his lawful son."

Miss Anastasia did not say a word; she bowed down her face upon her hands—that face over which an ashy paleness came slowly stealing like a cloud. Mrs Atheling hastened forward, thinking she was about to faint, but was put aside by a gesture. Then the colour came back, and Miss Anastasia rose up, herself again, with all her old energy.

"You are perfectly right, young Atheling—quite right—as you have always been," said Miss Rivers; "and, of course, you have told me in your letters the most part of what you could tell me now. But your boy is born for the law, Will Atheling," she said, turning suddenly to Charlie's pleased and admiring father. "He wrote to me as if I were a lawyer instead of a woman: all facts and no opinion; that was scant measure for me. Shake hands, boy. I'll see everything in the morning, and then we'll think of beginning the campaign. I have it in my head already—please Heaven! Charlie, we'll chase them from the field."

So saying, Miss Anastasia marched with an exultant and jubilant step, following Mrs Atheling up the narrow stairs. She was considerably shaken out of her usual composure—swells of great triumph, suddenly calmed by the motion of a moved heart, passed over the spirit of this brave old gentlewoman like sun and wind; and her self-appointed charge of the rights of her father's children, who might have been her own children so far as age was concerned, had a very singular effect upon her. Mrs Atheling did not linger a minute longer than she could help with her distinguished guest. She was proud of Miss Anastasia, but far prouder of Charlie,—Charlie, who had been a boy a little while ago, but who had come back a man.

"Come here and sit down, mother," said Charlie; "now we're by ourselves, if you will not tell the girls, I'll tell you everything. First, there's the marriage. That she belonged to the family I wrote of—the family Remori—I got at after a long time. She was an only daughter, and had no one to look after her. I have a certificate of the marriage, and a witness coming who was present—old Doctor Serrano—one of your patriots who is always in mischief; besides that, what do you think is my evidence for the marriage?"

"Indeed, Charlie, I could not guess," cried Mrs Atheling.

"There's a kind of tomb near the town, a thing as like the mausoleum at Winterbourne as possible, and quite as ugly. There is this good in ugliness," said Charlie, "that one remarks it, especially in Italy. I thought no one but an Englishman could have put up such an affair as that, and I could not make out one way or another who it belonged to, or what it was. The priests are very strong out there. They would not let a heretic lie in consecrated ground, and no one cared to go near this grave, if it was a grave. They wouldn't allow even that. You know what the Winterbourne tomb is—a great open canopied affair, with that vast flat stone below. There was a flat stone in the other one too, not half so big, and it looked to me as if it would lift easily enough. So what do you think I did? I made friends with some wild fellows about, and got hold of one young Englishman, and as soon as it was dark we got picks and tools and went off to the grave."

"Oh, Charlie!" Mrs Atheling turned very pale.

"After a lot of work we got it open," said Charlie, going on with great zest and animation. "Then the young fellow and I got down into the vault—a regular vault, where there had been a lamp suspended. *It*, I suppose, had gone out many a year ago; and there we found upon the two coffin-lids—well, it's very pitiful, mother, it is indeed—but we wanted it for evidence—on one of the coffins was this inscription:—'Giulietta Rivers, Lady Winterbourne, *née* Remori, died January 1822, aged twenty years.' If it had been a diamond mine it would not have given so much pleasure to me."

"Pleasure! oh Charlie!" cried Mrs Atheling faintly.

"But they might say *you* put it there, Charlie, and that it was not true," said Mr Atheling, who rather piqued himself upon his caution.

"That was what I had the other young fellow for," said Charlie quietly; "and that was what made me quite sure she belonged to the Remoris; it was easy enough after that—and I want only one link now, that is, to make sure of their identity. Father, do you remember anything about the children when they came to the Hall?"

Mr Atheling shook his head. "Your aunt Bridget, if she had been alive, would have been sure to know," said Mamma meditatively; "but Louis found out some old servant lately that had been about Winterbourne long ago."

"Louis! does he know?" cried Charlie.

"He is doing something on his own account, inquiring everything he can about Lord Winterbourne. He does not know, but guesses every possible kind of thing, except the truth," said Mr Atheling; "how long he may be of lighting upon that, it is impossible to say."

"Now Charlie, my dear boy, you can ask all about Louis to-morrow," said Mrs Atheling. "Louis! Dear me, William, to think of us calling him Louis, and treating him like any common young man, and he Lord Winterbourne all the time! and all through Charlie!—and oh, my Marian! when I think of it all, it bewilders me! But, Charlie, my dear, you must not be fatigued too much. Do not ask him any more questions to-night, papa; consider how important his health is; he must lie down directly. I'll make him all comfortable; and, William, do you go to the parlour—bid him good-night."

Papa obeyed, as dutiful papas are wont to obey, and Charlie laughed, but submitted, as his mother, with her own kind unwearying hands, arranged for him the sofa in the best room; for the Tyrolese and Miss Anastasia occupied all the available bedrooms in the house. Then she bade him good-night, drawing back his dark elf-locks, and kissing his forehead tenderly, and with a certain respect for the big boy who was a boy no longer; and then the good mother went away to arrange her husband similarly on the other sofa, and to take possession, last of all, of the easy-chair. "I can sleep in the day if I am disposed," said Mrs Atheling, who never was disposed for any such indulgence; and she leaned back in the big chair, with a mind disturbed and glowing, agitated with grand fancies. Marian! was it possible? But then, Agnes—after all, what a maze of splendid uncertainty it was!

CHAPTER XXIII
PROCRASTINATION

"You may say what you like, young Atheling," said Miss Rivers, "you've a very good right to your own opinion; but I'm not a lawyer, nor bound by rule and precedent, mind. This is the middle of March; *it* comes on in April; we must wait for that; and you're not up with all your evidence, you dilatory boy."

"But I might happen to be up with it in a day," said Charlie, "and at all events an ejectment should be served, and the first step taken in the case without delay."

"That is all very well," said the old lady, "but I don't suppose it would advance the business very much, besides rousing him at once to use every means possible, and perhaps buy off that poor old Serrano, or get hold of Monte. Why did you not look for Monte, young Atheling? The chances are that he was present too?"

"One witness was as much as I could manage," said Charlie, shrugging his shoulders at the recollection; "but the most important question of all—Louis—I mean—your brother—the heir—"

"My brother—the heir." Miss Rivers coloured suddenly. It was a different thing thinking of him in private, and hearing him spoken of so. "I tell you he is not the heir, young Atheling; he is Lord Winterbourne: but I will not see him yet, not till *the day*; it would be a terrible time of suspense for the poor boy."

"Then, if it is your pleasure, he must go away," said Charlie, firmly—"he cannot come here to this agitated house of ours without discovering a good deal of the truth; and if he discovered it so, he would have just grounds to complain. If he is not told at once, he ought to have some commission such as I have had, and be sent away."

Miss Rivers coloured still more, all her liking for Charlie and his family scarcely sufficing to reconcile her to the "sending away" of the young heir, on the same footing as she had sent young Atheling. She hesitated and faltered visibly, seeing reason enough in it, but extremely repugnant. "If you think so," she said at last, with a slightly averted face, "ah—another time we can speak of that."

Then came further consultations, and Charlie had to tell his story over bit by bit, and incident by incident, illustrating every point of it by his documents. Miss Anastasia was particularly anxious about the young Englishman whose name was signed with Charlie's own, in certification of the inscription on the coffin. Miss Anastasia marvelled much whether he belonged to the Hillarys of Lincolnshire, or the Hillarys of Yorkshire, and pursued his shadow through half-a-dozen counties. Charlie was not particularly given to genealogy. He had the young man's card, with his address at the Albany, and the time of his possible return home. That was quite enough for the matter in hand, and Charlie was very much more concerned about the one link wanting in his evidence—the person who received the children from the care of Leonore the Tyrolese.

As it chanced, in this strange maze of circumstance, the Rector chose this day for one of his visits. He was very much amazed to encounter Miss Anastasia; it struck him evidently as something which needed to be accounted for, for she was known and noted as a dweller at home. She received him at first with a certain triumphant satisfaction, but by-and-by a little confusion appeared even in the looks of Miss Anastasia. She began to glance from the stately young man to the pale face and drooping eyelids of Agnes. She began to see the strange mixture of trouble and hardship in this extraordinary revolution, and her heart was touched for the heir deposed, as well as for the heir discovered. Lionel was "in trouble" himself, after an odd enough fashion. Some one had just instituted an action against him in the ecclesiastical courts touching the furniture of his altar, and the form in which he conducted the services. It was a strange poetic justice to bring this against him now, when he himself had cast off his high-churchism, and was luxuriating in his new freedom. But the Curate grew perfectly inspired under the infliction, and rose to the highest altitude of satisfaction and happiness, declaring this to be the testing-touch of persecution, which constantly distinguishes the true faith. It was on Miss Anastasia's lips to speak of this, and to ask the young clergyman why he was so long away from home at so critical a juncture, but her heart was touched with compunction. From looking at Lionel, she turned suddenly to Agnes, and asked, with a strange abruptness, a question which had no connection with the previous conversation—"That little book of yours, Agnes Atheling, that you sent to me, what do you mean by that story, child?—eh?—what put *that* into your idle little brain? It is not like fiction; it is quite as strange and out of the way as if it had been life."

Involuntarily Agnes lifted her heavy eyelids, and cast a shy look of distress and sympathy upon the unconscious Rector, who never missed any look of hers, but could not tell what this meant. "I do not know," said Agnes; but the question did not wake the shadow of a smile upon her face—it rather made her resentful. She thought it cruel of Miss Anastasia, now that all doubt was over, and Lionel was certainly disinherited. Disinherited!—he had never possessed anything actual, and nothing was taken from him; whereas Louis had been defrauded of his rights all his life; but Agnes instinctively took the part of the present sufferer—the unwitting sufferer, who suspected no evil.

But the Rector was startled in his turn by the question of Miss Anastasia. It revived in his own mind the momentary conviction of reality with which he had read the little book. When Miss Anastasia turned away for a moment, he addressed Agnes quietly aside, making a kind of appeal. "Had you, then, a real foundation—is it a true tale?" he said, looking at her with a little anxiety. She glanced up at him again, with her eyes so full of distress, anxiety, warning—then looked down with a visible paleness and trembling, faltered very much in her answer, and at last only said, expressing herself with difficulty, "It is not all real—only something like a story I have heard."

But Agnes could not bear his inquiring look; she hastily withdrew to the other side of the room, eager to be out of reach of the eyes which followed her everywhere. For his part, Lionel's first idea was of some distress of hers, which he instinctively claimed the right to soothe; but the thing remained in his mind, and gave him a certain vague uneasiness; he read the book over again when he went home, to make it out if he could, but fell so soon into thought of the writer, and consideration of that sweet youthful voice of hers, that there was no coming to any light in the matter. He not only gave it up, but forgot it again, only marvelling what was the mystery which looked so sorrowful and so bright out of Agnes Atheling's eyes.

They all waited with some little apprehension that night for the visit of Louis. He was very late; the evening wore away, and Miss Anastasia had long ago departed, taking with her, to the satisfaction of every one, the voluble Tyrolese; but Louis was not to be seen nor heard of. Very late, as they were all preparing for rest, some one came to the door. The knock raised a sudden colour on the cheeks of Marian, which had grown very pale for an hour or two. But it was not Louis; it was, however, a note from him, which Marian ran up-stairs to read. She came down again a moment after, with a pale face, painfully keeping in two big tears. "Oh, mamma, he has gone away," said Marian. She did not want to cry, and it was impossible to speak without crying; and yet she did not like to confide to any one the lover's letter. At last the tears fell, and Marian found her voice. He had just heard suddenly something very important, had seen Mr Foggo about it, and had hurried off to the country; he would not be detained long, he was sure; he had not a moment to explain anything, but would write whenever he got there. "He does not even say where," said Marian, sadly; and Rachel came close up to her, and cried without any restraint, as Marian very much wished, but did not quite like to do before her father and her brother. Mrs Atheling took them both into a corner, and scolded them after a fashion she had. "My dears, do you think you cannot trust Louis?" said Mamma— "nonsense!—we shall hear to-morrow morning. Why, he has spoken to Mr Foggo, and you may be quite sure everything is right, and that it was the most sensible thing he could do."

But it was very odd certainly, not at all explainable, and withal the most seasonable thing in the world. "I should think it quite a providence," said Mrs Atheling, "if we only heard where he was."

CHAPTER XXIV
THE FOGGOS

The first thing to be done in the morning, before it was time even for the postman, was to hasten to Killiecrankie Lodge, and ascertain all that could be ascertained concerning Louis from Mr Foggo. This mission was confided to Agnes. It was a soft spring-like morning, and the first of Miss Willsie's wallflowers were beginning to blow. Miss Willsie herself was walking in her little garden, scattering crumbs upon the gravel-path for the poor dingy town-sparrows, and the stray robin whom some unlucky wind had blown to Bellevue. But Miss Willsie was disturbed out of her usual equanimity; she looked a little heated, as if she had come here to recover herself, and rather frightened her little feathered acquaintances by the vehemence with which she threw them her daily dole. She smoothed her brow a little at sight of Agnes. "And what may *you* be wanting at such an hour as this?" said Miss Willsie; "if there is one thing I cannot bide, it is to see young folk wandering about, without any errand, at all the hours of the day!"

"But I have an errand," said Agnes. "I want to ask Mr Foggo about—about Mr Louis—if he knows where he has gone!"

Mr Louis—his surname, as everybody supposed—was the name by which Louis was known in Bellevue.

Miss Willsie's brow puckered with a momentary anger. "I would like to know," said Miss Willsie, "why that monkey could not content herself with a kindly lad at home: but my brother's in the parlour; you'll find him there, Agnes. Keep my patience!—Foggie's there too—the lad from America. If there's one thing in this world I cannot endure, it's just a young man like yon!"

Miss Willsie, however, reluctantly followed her young visitor into the breakfast parlour, from which the old lady had lately made an indignant and unceremonious exit. It was a very comfortable breakfast-table, fully deserving the paragraph it obtained in those "Letters from England," which are so interesting to all the readers of the *Mississippi Gazette*. There was a Scottish prodigality of creature comforts, and the fine ancient table-linen was white as snow, and there was a very unusual abundance, for a house of this class, of heavy old plate. Mr Foggo was getting through his breakfast methodically, with the *Times* erected before him, and forming a screen between himself and his worshipful nephew; while Mr Foggo S. Endicott, seated with a due regard to his profile, at such an angle with the light as to exhibit fitly that noble outline, conveyed his teacup a very long way up from the table, at dignified intervals, to his handsome and expressive mouth.

Agnes hastened to the elder gentleman at once, and drew him aside to make her inquiries. Mr Foggo smiled, and took a pinch of snuff. "All quite true," said Mr Foggo; "he came to me yesterday with a paper in his hand—a long story about next of kin wanted somewhere, and of two children belonging to some poor widow woman, who had been lost sight of a long time ago, one of whom was named Louis. That's the story; it's a mare's nest, Agnes, if you know what that is; but I thought it might divert the boy; so instead of opposing, I furnished him for his journey, and let him go without delay. No reason why the lad should not do his endeavour for his own hand. It's good for him, though it's sure to be a failure. He has told you perfectly true."

"And where has he gone?" asked Agnes anxiously.

"It's in one of the midland counties—somewhere beyond Birmingham— at this moment I do not remember the place," said Mr Foggo; "but I took a note of it, and you'll hear from him to-morrow. We've been hearing news ourselves, Agnes. Did you tell her, Willsie, what fortune has come to you and me?"

"No," said Miss Willsie. She was turning her back upon her dutiful nephew, and frowning darkly upon the teapot. The American had no chance with his offended aunt.

"A far-away cousin of ours," said Mr Foggo, who was very bland, and in a gracious humour, "has taken it into his head to die; and a very bonny place indeed, in the north country—a cosy little estate and a good house— comes to me."

"I am very glad," said Agnes, brightening in sympathy; "that is good news for everybody. Oh, Miss Willsie, how pleased Mr Foggo must be!"

Miss Willsie did not say a word—Mr Foggo smiled. "Then you think a cosy estate a good thing, Agnes?" said the old gentleman. "I am rather afraid, though you write books, you are not poetical; for that is not the view of the subject taken by my nephew here."

"I despise wealth," said Mr Endicott. "An estate, sir, is so much dirty soil. The mind is the true riches; a spark of genius is worth all the inheritances in the world!"

"And that's just so much the better for you, Foggie, my man," cried Miss Willsie suddenly; "seeing the inheritances of this world are very little like to come to your share. If there's one thing I hate, it's a lee!"

Mr Endicott took no notice of this abstract deliverance. "A very great estate—the ancient feudal domain—the glens and the gorges of the Highland chief, I respect, sir," said the elevated Yankee; "but a man who can influence a thousand minds—a man whose course is followed eagerly by the eyes of half a nation—such a man is not likely to be tempted to envy by a mile of indifferent territory. My book, by which I can move a world, is my lever of Archimedes; this broadsheet"—and he laid his hand upon the pages of the *Mississippi Gazette*—"is my kingdom! Miss Atheling, I shall have the honour of paying my respects to your family to-day. I shall soon take leave of Europe. I have learned much—I have experienced much—I am rejoiced to think I have been able to throw some light upon the manners and customs of your people; and henceforward I intend to devote myself to the elucidation of my own."

"We shall be very glad to see you, Mr Endicott," said Agnes, who was rather disposed to take his part, seeing he stood alone. "Now I must hasten home and tell them. We were all very anxious; but every one will be glad, Mr Foggo, to hear of you. We shall feel as if the good fortune had come to ourselves."

"Ay, Agnes, and so it might, if Marian, silly monkey, had kept a thought for one that liked her well," said Miss Willsie, as she went with her young visitor. "Poor Harry! his uncle's heart yearns to him; *our* gear will never go the airt of a fool like yon!" said Miss Willsie, growing very Scotch and very emphatic, as she inclined her head in the direction of Mr Endicott; "but Harry will be little heeding who gets the siller *now*."

Poor Harry! since he had heard of *it*—since he had known of Marian's engagement, he had never had the heart to make a single appearance in Bellevue.

Mr Endicott remembered his promise; he went forth in state, as soon after noon as he could go, with a due regard to the proper hour for a morning call. Mr Endicott, though he had endured certain exquisite pangs of jealousy, was not afraid of Louis; he could not suppose that any one was so blind, having *his* claims fairly placed before them, as to continue to prefer another; such an extent of human perversity did not enter into the calculations of Mr Endicott. And he was really "in love," like the rest of these young people. All the readers of the *Mississippi Gazette* knew of a certain lovely face, which brightened the imagination of their "representative man," and it was popularly expected on the other side of the water, in those refined circles familiar with Mr Endicott, that he was about to bring his bride home. He had an additional stimulus from this expectation, and went forth to-day with the determination of securing Marian Atheling. He was a little nervous, because there was a good deal of real emotion lying at the bottom of his heart; but, after all, was more doubtful of getting an opportunity than of the answer which should follow when the opportunity was gained.

To his extreme amazement, he found Marian alone. He understood it in a moment—they had left her on purpose—they comprehended his intentions! She was pale, her beautiful eyes glistened, and were wet and dewy. Perhaps she, too, had an intuition of what was coming. He thought her subdued manner, the tremble in her voice, the eyes, which were cast down so often, and did not care to meet his full gaze, were all signs of that maiden consciousness about which he had written many a time. In the full thought of this, the eloquent young American dispensed with all preamble. He came to her side with the delightful benevolence of a lover who could put this beautiful victim of his fascinations out of her suspense at once. He addressed her by her name—he added the most endearing words he could think of—he took her hand. The young beauty started from him absolutely with violence. "What do you mean, sir?" said Marian. Then she stood erect at a little distance, her eyes flashing, her cheek burning, holding her hands tight together, with an air of petulant and angry defiance. Mr Endicott was thunderstruck. "Did you not expect me—do you not understand me?" said the lover, not yet daunted. "Pardon me; I have shocked your delicate feelings. You cannot think I mean to do it, Marian, sweet British rose? You know me too well for that; you know my mind—you appreciate my feelings. You were born to be a poet's bride—I come to offer you a poet's heart!"

Before he had concluded, Marian recovered herself; into the dewy eyes, that had been musing upon Louis, the old light of girlish mischief came arch and sweet. "I did not quite understand you, Mr Endicott," said Marian, demurely. "You alarmed me a little; but I am very much obliged, and you are very good; only, I—I am sorry. I suppose you do not know I—I am engaged!"

She said this with a bright blush, casting down her eyes. She thought, after all, it was the honestest and the easiest fashion of dismissing her new lover.

"Engaged! Marian, you did not know of me—you were not acquainted with my sentiments," cried the American. "Oh, for a miserable dream of honour, will you blight my life and your own? You were not aware of my love—you were ignorant of my devotion. Beautiful Mayflower! you are free of what you did in ignorance—you are free for me!"

Marian snatched away her hand again with resentment. "I suppose you do not mean to be very impertinent, Mr Endicott, but you are so," cried the indignant little beauty. "I do not like you—I never did like you. I am very sorry, indeed, if you really cared for me. If I were free a hundred times over—if I never had seen any one," cried Marian vehemently, blushing with sudden passion, and feeling disposed to cry, "I never could have had anything to say to you. Mamma—oh, I am sure it is very cruel!—Mamma, will you speak to Mr Endicott? He has been very rude to me!"

Mamma, who came in at the moment out of the garden, started with amazement to see the flushed cheeks of Marian, and Mr Endicott, who stood in an appealing attitude, with the most crestfallen and astonished face. Marian ran from the room in an instant, scarcely able to restrain her tears of vexation and annoyance, till she was out of sight. Mrs Atheling placed a chair for her daughter's suitor very solemnly. "What has happened?—what have you been saying, Mr Endicott?" said the indignant mother.

"I have only been offering to your daughter's acceptance all that a man has to offer," said the American, with a little real dignity. "It is over; the young lady has made her own election—she rejects *me*! It is well! it is but another depth of human suffering opening to *his* feet who must tread them all! But I have nothing to apologise for. Madam, farewell!"

"Oh, stay a moment! I am very sorry—she is so young. I am sure she did not mean to offend you," said Mrs Atheling, with distress. "She is engaged, Mr Endicott. Miss Willsie knew of it. I am sure I am grieved if the foolish child has answered you unkindly; but she is engaged."

"So I am aware, madam," said Mr Endicott, gloomily; "may it be for her happiness—may no poetic retribution attend her! As for me, my art is my lifelong consolation. This, even, is for the benefit of the world; do not concern yourself for me."

But Mrs Atheling hastened up-stairs when he was gone, to reprove her daughter. To her surprise, Marian defended herself with spirit. "He was impertinent, mamma," said Marian; "he said if I had known he cared for me, I would not have been engaged. He! when everybody knows I never would speak to him. It was he who insulted me!"

So Mr Endicott's English romance ended, after all, in a paragraph which, when the time comes, we shall feel a melancholy pleasure in transcribing from the eloquent pages of the *Mississippi Gazette*.

CHAPTER XXV
GOOD FORTUNE

This evening was extremely quiet, and something dull, to the inhabitants of Bellevue. Though everybody knew of the little adventure of Mr Endicott, the young people were all too reverential of the romance of youth themselves to laugh very freely at the disappointed lover. Charlie sat by himself in the best room, sedulously making out his case. Charlie had risen into a person of great importance at the office since his return, and, youth as he was, was trusted so far, under Mr Foggo's superintendence, as to draw up the brief for the counsel who was to conduct this great case; so they had not even his presence to enliven the family circle, which was very dull without Louis. Then Agnes, for her part, had grown daily more self-occupied; Mrs Atheling pondered over this, half understood it, and did not ask a question on the subject. She glanced very often at the side-table, where her elder daughter sat writing. This was not a common evening occupation with Agnes; but she found a solace in that making of fables, and was forth again, appealing earnestly, with all the power and privilege of her art, not so much to her universal audience as to one among them, who by-and-by might find out the second meaning—the more fervent personal voice.

As for Marian and Rachel, they both sat at work somewhat melancholy, whispering to each other now and then, speaking low when they spoke to any one else. Papa was at his newspaper, reading little bits of news to them; but even Papa was cloudy, and there was a certain shade of dulness and melancholy over all the house.

Some one came to the door when the evening was far advanced, and held a long parley with Susan; the issue of which was, that Susan made her appearance in the parlour to ask information. "A man, ma'am, that Mr Louis appointed to come to him to-night," said Susan, "and he wants to know, please, when Mr Louis is coming home."

Mrs Atheling went to the door to answer the inquiry; then, having become somewhat of a plotter herself by force of example, she bethought her of calling Charlie. The man was brought into the best room; he was an ordinary-looking elderly man, like a small shopkeeper. He stated what he wanted slowly, without any of the town sharpness. He said the young gentleman was making out some account—as he understood—about Lord Winterbourne, and hearing that he had been once about the Hall in his young days, had come to him to ask some questions. He was a likely young gentleman, and summat in his own mind told the speaker he had seen his face afore, whether it were about the Hall, or where it were, deponent did not know; but thinking upon it, just bethought him at this moment that he was mortal like the old lord. Now the young gentleman—as he heard—had gone sudden away to the country, and the lady of the house where he lived had sent the perplexed caller here.

"I know very well about that quarter myself," said Mrs Atheling. "Do you know the Old Wood Lodge? that belongs to us; and if you have friends in the village, I daresay I shall know your name."

The man put up his hand to his forehead respectfully. "I knowed the old lady at the Lodge many a year ago," said he. "My name's John Morrall. I was no more nor a helper at the stables in my day; and a sister of mine had charge of some children about the Hall."

"Some children—who were they?" said Charlie. "Perhaps Lord Winterbourne's children; but that would be very long ago."

"Well, sir," said the man with a little confusion, glancing aside at Mrs Atheling, "saving the lady's presence, I'd be bold to say that they was my lord's, but in a sort of an—unlawful way; two poor little morsels of twins, that never had nothing like other children. He wasn't any way kind to them, wasn't my lord."

"I think I know the children you mean," said Charlie, to the surprise and admiration of his mother, who checked accordingly the exclamation on her own lips. "Do you know where they came from?—were you there when they were brought to the Hall?"

"Ay, sir, *I* know—no man better," said Morrall. "Sally was the woman— all along of my lord's man that she was keeping company with the same time, little knowing, poor soul, what she was to come to—that brought them unfortunate babbies out of London. I don't know no more. Sally's opinion was, they came out o' foreign parts afore that; for the nurse they had with them, Sally said, was some outlandish kind of a Portugee."

"A Portuguese!" exclaimed both the listeners in dismay—but Charlie added immediately, "What made your sister suppose she was a Portuguese?"

"Well, sir, she was one of them foreign kind of folks—but noways like my lady's French maid, Sally said—so taking thought what she was, a cousin of ours that's a sailor made no doubt but she was a Portugee—so she gave up the little things to Sally, not one of them able to say a word to each other; for the foreign woman, poor soul, knew no English, and Sally brought down the babbies to the Hall."

"Does your sister live at Winterbourne?" asked Charlie.

"What, Sally, sir? poor soul!" said John Morrall, "to her grief she married my lord's man, again all we could say, and he went pure to the bad, as was to be seen of him, and listed—and now she's off in Ireland with the regiment, a poor creature as you could see—five children, ma'am, alive, and she's had ten; always striving to do her best, but never able, poor soul, to keep a decent gown to her back."

"Will you tell me where she is?" said Charlie, while his mother went hospitably away to bring a glass of wine, a rare and unusual dainty, for the refreshment of this most welcome visitor—"there is an inquiry going on at present, and her evidence might be of great value: it will be good for her, don't fear. Let me know where she is."

While Charlie took down the address, his mother, with her own hand, served Mr John Morrall with a slice of cake and a comfortable glass of port-wine. "But I am sure you are comfortable yourself—you look so, at least."

"I am in the green-grocery trade," said their visitor, putting up his hand again with "his respects," "and got a good wife and three as likely childer as a man could desire. It ain't just as easy as it might be keeping all things square, but we always get on; and lord! if folks had no crosses, they'd ne'er know they were born. Look at Sally, there's a picture!—and after that, says I, it don't become such like as us to complain."

Finally, having finished his refreshment, and left his own address with a supplementary note, and touch of the forehead—"It ain't very far off; glad to serve you, ma'am"—Mr John Morrall withdrew. Then Charlie returned to his papers, but not quite so composedly as usual. "Put up my travelling-bag, mother," said Charlie, after a few ineffectual attempts to resume; "I'll not write any more to-night; it's just nine o'clock. I'll step over and see old Foggo, and be off to Ireland to-morrow, without delay."

CHAPTER XXVI
THE OXFORD ASSIZES

April, as cloudless and almost as warm as summer, a day when all the spring was swelling sweet in all the young buds and primroses, and the broad dewy country smiled and glistened under the rising of that sun, which day by day shone warmer and fuller on the woods and on the fields. But the point of interest was not the country; it was not a spring festival which drew so many interested faces along the high-road. An expectation not half so amiable was abroad among the gentry of Banburyshire—a great many people, quite an unusual crowd, took their way to the spring assizes to listen to a trial which was not at all important on its own account. The defendants were not even known among the county people, nor was there much curiosity about them. It was a family quarrel which roused the kind and amiable expectations of all these excellent people,—The Honourable Anastasia Rivers against Lord Winterbourne. It was popularly anticipated that Miss Anastasia herself was to appear in the witness-box, and everybody who knew the belligerents, delighted at the prospect of mischief, hastened to be present at the fight.

And there was a universal gathering, besides, of all the people more immediately interested in this beginning of the war. Lord Winterbourne himself, with a certain ghastly levity in his demeanour, which sat ill upon his bloodless face, and accorded still worse with the mourner's dress which he wore, graced the bench. Charlie Atheling sat in his proper place below, as agent for the defendant, within reach of the counsel for the same. His mother and sisters were with Miss Anastasia, in a very favourable place for seeing and hearing; the Rector was not far from them, very much interested, but exceedingly surprised at the unchanging paleness of Agnes, and the obstinacy with which she refused to meet his eye; for that she avoided him, and seemed overwhelmed by some secret and uncommunicated mystery, which no one else, even in her own family, shared, was clear enough to a perception quickened by the extreme "interest" which Lionel Rivers felt in Agnes Atheling. Even Rachel had been brought thither in the train of

Miss Anastasia; and though rather disturbed by her position, and by the disagreeable and somewhat terrifying consciousness of being observed by Lord Winterbourne, in whose presence she had not been before, since the time she left the Hall—Rachel, with her veil over her face, had a certain timid enjoyment of the bustle and novelty of the scene. Louis, too, was there, sent down on the previous night with a commission from Mr Foggo; there was no one wanting. The two or three who knew the tactics of the day, awaited their disclosure with great secret excitement, speculating upon their effect; and those who did not, looked on eagerly with interest and anxiety and hope.

Only Agnes sat drawing back from them, between her mother and sister, letting her veil hang with a pitiful unconcern in thick double folds half over her pale face. She did not care to lift her eyes; she looked heavy, wretched, spiritless; she could not keep her thoughts upon the smiling side of the picture; she thought only of the sudden blow about to fall—of the bitter sense of deception and craftiness, of the overwhelming disappointment which this day must bring forth.

The case commenced. Lord Winterbourne's counsel stated the plea of his noble client; it did not occupy a very long time, for no one supposed it very important. The statement was, that Miss Bridget Atheling had been presented by the late Lord Winterbourne with a life-interest in the little property involved; that the Old Wood Lodge, the only property in the immediate neighbourhood which was not in the peaceful possession of Lord Winterbourne, had never been separated or alienated from the estate; that, in fact, the gift to Miss Bridget was a mere tenant's claim upon the house during her lifetime, with no power of bequest whatever; and the present Lord Winterbourne's toleration of its brief occupancy by the persons in possession, was merely a good-humoured carelessness on the part of his lordship of a matter not sufficiently important to occupy his thoughts. The only evidence offered was the distinct enumeration of the Old Wood Lodge along with the Old Wood House, and the cottages in the village of Winterbourne, as in possession of the family at the accession of the late lord; and the learned gentleman concluded his case by declaring that he confidently challenged his opponent to produce any deed or document whatever which so much as implied that the property had been bestowed upon Bridget Atheling. No deed of gift—no conveyance—nothing whatever in the shape of title-deeds, he was confident, existed to support the claim of the defendant; a claim which, if it was not a direct attempt to profit by the inadvertence of his noble client, was certainly a very ugly and startling mistake.

So far everything was brief enough, and conclusive enough, as it appeared. The audience was decidedly disappointed: if the answer was after this style, there was no "fun" to be expected, and it had been an entire hoax which seduced the Banburyshire notabilities to waste the April afternoon in a crowded court-house. But Miss Anastasia, swelling with anxiety and yet with triumph, was visible to every one; visible also to one eye was something very different — Agnes, pale, shrinking, closing her eyes, looking as if she would faint. The Rector made his way behind, and spoke to her anxiously. He was afraid she was ill; could he assist her through the crowd? Agnes turned her face to him for a moment, and her eyes, which looked so dilated and pitiful, but only said "No, no," in a hurried whisper, and turned again. The counsel on the other side had risen, and was about to begin the defence.

"My learned brother is correct, and doubtless knows himself to be so," said the advocate of the Athelings. "We have no deed to produce, though we have something nearly as good; but, my lord, I am instructed suddenly to change the entire ground of my plea. Certain information which has come to the knowledge of my clients, but which it was not their wish to make public at present, has been now communicated to me; and I beg to object at once to the further progress of the suit, on a ground which your lordship will at once acknowledge to be just and forcible. I assert that the present bearer of the title is not the true Lord Winterbourne."

There rose immediately a hum and murmur of the strangest character — not applause, not disapproval — simple consternation, so extreme that no one could restrain its utterance. People rose up and stared at the speaker, as if he had been seized with sudden madness in their presence; then there ensued a scene of much tumult and agitation. The judges on the bench interposed indignantly. The counsel for Lord Winterbourne sprang to his feet, appealing with excitement to their lordships — was this to be permitted? Even the audience, Lord Winterbourne's neighbours, who had no love for him, pressed forward as if to support him in this crisis, and with resentment and disapproval looked upon Miss Anastasia, to whom every one turned instinctively, as to a conspirator who had overshot the mark. It was scarcely possible for the daring speaker to gain himself a hearing. When he did so, at last, it was rather as a culprit than an accuser. But even the frown of a chief-justice did not appal a man who held Charlie Atheling's papers in his hands; he was heard again, declaring, with force and dignity, that he was incapable of making such a statement without proofs in his possession which put it beyond controversy. He begged but a moment's patience, in justice to himself and to his client, while he placed an abstract of the case and the evidence in their lordships' hands.

Then to the sudden hum and stir, which the officials of the court had not been able to put down, succeeded that total, strange, almost appalling stillness of a crowd, which is so very impressive at all times. While the judges consulted together, looking keenly over these mysterious papers, almost every eye among the spectators was riveted upon them. No one noticed even Lord Winterbourne, who stood up in his place unconsciously, overlooking them all, quite unaware of the prominence and singularity of his position, gazing before him with a motionless blank stare, like a man looking into the face of Fate. The auditors waited almost breathless for the decision of the law. That anything so wild and startling could ever be taken into consideration by those grave authorities was of itself extraordinary; and as the consultation was prolonged, the anxiety grew gradually greater. Could there be reality in it? could it be true?

At last the elder judge broke the silence. "This is a very serious statement," he said: "of course, it involves issues much more important than the present question. As further proceedings will doubtless be grounded on these documents, it is our opinion that the hearing of this case had better be adjourned."

Lord Winterbourne seated himself when he heard the voice—it broke the spell; but not so Louis, who stood beneath, alone, looking straight up at the speaker in his judicial throne. The truth flashed to the mind of Louis like a gleam of lightning. He did not ask a question, though Charlie was close by him; he did not turn his head, though Miss Anastasia was within reach of his eye; his whole brain seemed to burn and glow; the veins swelled upon his forehead; he raised up his head for air, for breath, like a man overwhelmed; he did not see how the gaze of half the assembly began to be attracted to himself. In this sudden pause he stood still, following out the conviction which burst upon him—this conviction, which suddenly, like a sunbeam, made all things clear. Wrong as he had been in the details, his imagination was true as the most unerring judgment. For what child in the world was it so much this man's interest to disgrace and disable as the child whose rights he usurped—his brother's lawful heir? This silence was like a lifetime to Louis, but it ended in a moment. Some confused talking followed—objections on the part of Lord Winterbourne's representative, which were overruled; and then another case was called—a common little contest touching mere lands and houses—and every one awoke, as at the touch of a disenchanting rod, to the common pale daylight and common controversy, as from a dream.

Then the people streamed out in agitated groups, some retaining their first impulse of contradiction and resentment; others giving up at once, and receiving the decision of the judges as final. Then Agnes looked back, with a sick and trembling anxiety, for the Rector. The Rector was gone; and they all followed one after another, silent in the great tremor of their excitement. When they came to the open air, Marian began to ask questions eagerly, and Rachel to cry behind her veil, and cast woeful wistful looks at Miss Anastasia. What was it? what was the matter? was it anything about Louis? who was Lord Winterbourne?

CHAPTER XXVII
THE TRUE HEIR

"I do not know how he takes it, mother," said Charlie. "I do not know if he takes it at all; he has not spoken a single word all the way home."

He did not seem disposed to speak many now; he went into Miss Bridget's dusky little parlour, lingering a moment at the door, and bending forward in reflection from the little sloping mirror on the wall. The young man was greatly moved, silent with inexpressible emotion; he went up to Marian first, and, in the presence of them all, kissed her little trembling hand and her white cheek; then he drew her forward with him, holding her up with his own arm, which trembled too, and came direct to Miss Anastasia, who was seated, pale, and making gigantic efforts to command herself, in old Miss Bridget's chair. "This is my bride," said Louis firmly, yet with quivering lips. "What are we to call *you*?"

The old lady looked at him for a moment, vainly endeavouring to retain her self-possession—then sprang up suddenly, grasped him in her arms, and broke forth into such a cry of weeping as never had been heard before under this peaceful roof. "What you will! what you will! my boy, my heir, my father's son!" cried Miss Anastasia, lifting up her voice. No one moved, or spoke a word—it was like one of those old agonies of thanksgiving in the old Scriptures, when a Joseph or a Jacob, parted for half a patriarch's lifetime, "fell upon his neck and wept."

When this moment of extreme agitation was over, the principal actors in the family drama came again into a moderate degree of calmness: Louis was almost solemn in his extreme youthful gravity. The young man was changed in a moment, as, perhaps, nothing but this overwhelming flood of honour and prosperity could have changed him. He desired to see the evidence and investigate his own claims thoroughly, as it was natural he should; then he asked Charlie to go out with him, for there was not a great deal of room in this little house, for private conference. The two young men went forth together through those quiet well-known lanes, upon which Louis gazed with a giddy eye. "This should have come to me in some place where I was a stranger," he said with excitement; "it might have seemed more credible, more reasonable, in a less familiar place. Here, where I have been an outcast and dishonoured all my life—here!"

"Your own property," said Charlie. "I'm not a poetical man, you know—it is no use trying—but I'd come to a little sentiment, I confess, if I were you."

"In the mean time there are other people concerned," said Louis, taking Charlie's arm, and turning him somewhat hurriedly away from the edge of the wood, which at this epoch of his fortunes, the scene of so many despairing fancies, was rather more than he chose to experiment upon. "You are not poetical, Charlie. I do not suppose it has come to your turn yet—but we do not want poetry to-night; there are other people concerned. So far as I can see, your case—I scarcely can call it mine, who have had no hand in it—is clear as daylight—indisputable. Is it so?—you know better than me."

"Indisputable," said Charlie, authoritatively.

"Then it should never come to a trial—for the honour of the house— for pity," said the heir. "A bad man taken in the toils is a very miserable thing to look at, Charlie; let us spare him if we can. I should like you to get some one who is to be trusted—say Mr Foggo, with some well-known man along with him—to wait upon Lord Winterbourne. Let them go into the case fully, and show him everything: say that I am quite willing that the world should think he had done it in ignorance—and persuade him—that is, if he is convinced, and they have perfect confidence in the case. The story need not be publicly known. Is it practicable?—tell me at once."

"It's practicable if he'll do it," said Charlie; "but he'll not do it, that's all."

"How do you know he'll not do it?—it is to save himself," said Louis.

"If he had not known it all along, he'd have given in," said Charlie, "and taken your offer, of course; but he *has* known it all along—it's been his ghost for years. He has his plans all prepared and ready, you may be perfectly sure. It is generous of you to suggest such a thing, but *he* would suppose it a sign of weakness. Never mind that—it's not of the least importance what he supposes; if you desire it, we can try."

"I do desire it," said Louis; "and then, Charlie, there is the Rector."

Charlie shook his head regretfully. "I am sorry for him myself," said the young lawyer; "but what can you do?"

"He has been extremely kind to me," said Louis, with a slight trembling in his voice—"kinder than any one in the world, except your own family.

There is his house—I see what to do; let us go at once and explain everything to him to-night."

"To-night! that's premature—showing your hand," said Charlie, startled in his professional caution: "never mind, you can stand it; he's a fine fellow, though he is the other line. If you like it, I don't object; but what shall you say?"

"He ought to have his share," said Louis—"don't interrupt me, Charlie; it is more generous in our case to receive than to give. He ought, if I represent the elder branch, to have the younger's share: he ought to permit me to do as much for him as he would have done for me. Ah, he bade me look at the pictures to see that I was a Rivers. I did not suppose any miracle on earth could make me proud of the name."

They went on hastily together in the early gathering darkness. The Old Wood House stood blank and dull as usual, with all its closed blinds; but the gracious young Curate, meditating his sermon, and much elated by his persecution, was straying about the well-kept paths. Mr Mead hastened to tell them that Mr Rivers had left home—"hastened away instantly to appear in our own case," said the young clergyman. "The powers of this world are in array against us—we suffer persecution, as becomes the true church. The Rector left hurriedly to appear in person. He is a devoted man, a noble Anglican. I smile myself at the reproaches of our adversary; I have no fear."

"We may see him in town," said Louis, turning away with disappointment. "If you write, will you mention that I have been here to-night, to beg his counsel and friendship—I, Louis Rivers—" A sudden colour flushed over the young man's face; he pronounced the name with a nervous firmness; it was the first time he had called himself by any save his baptismal name all his life.

As they turned and walked home again, Louis relapsed into his first agitated consciousness, and did not care to say a word. Louis Rivers! lawful heir and only son of a noble English peer and an unsullied mother. It was little wonder if the young man's heart swelled within him, too high for a word or a thought. He blotted out the past with a generous haste, unwilling to remember a single wrong done to him in the time of his humiliation, and looked out upon the future as upon a glorious vision, almost too wonderful to be realised: it was best to rest in this agitated moment of strange triumph, humility, and power, to convince himself that this was real, and to project his anticipations forward only with a generous anxiety for the concerns of others, with no question, when all questions were so overwhelming and incredible, after this extraordinary fortune of his own.

CHAPTER XXVIII
AT HOME

It would not be easy to describe the state of mind of the feminine portion of this family which remained at home. Marian, in a strange and overpowering tumult—Marian, who was the first and most intimately concerned, her cheek burning still under the touch of her lover's trembling lip in that second and more solemn betrothal, sat on a stool, half hidden by Miss Anastasia's big chair and ample skirts, supporting her flushed cheeks on those pretty rose-tipped hands, to which the flush seemed to have extended, her beautiful hair drooping down among her fingers, her eyes cast down, her heart leaping like a bird against her breast. Her own vague suspicions, keen and eager as they were, had never pointed half so far as this. If it did not "turn her head" altogether, it was more because the little head was giddy with amaze and confusion, than from any virtue on the part of Marian. She was quite beyond the power of thinking; a strange brilliant extraordinary panorama glided before her—Louis in Bellevue—Louis at the Old Wood Lodge—Louis, the lord of all he looked upon, in Winterbourne Hall!

Rachel, for her part, was to be found, now in one corner, now in another, crying very heartily, and with a general vague impulse of kissing every one in the present little company with thanks and gratitude, and being caressed and sympathised with in turn. The only one here, indeed, who seemed in her full senses was Agnes, who kept them all in a certain degree of self-possession. It was all over, at last, after so long a time of suspense and mystery; Agnes was relieved of her secret knowledge. She was grave, but she did not refuse to participate in the confused joy and thankfulness of the house. Now that the secret was revealed, her mind returned to its usual tone. Though she had so much "interest" in Lionel—almost as much as he felt in her—she had too high a mind herself to suppose him overwhelmed by the single fact that his inheritance had passed away from him. When all was told, she breathed freely. She had all the confidence in him which one high heart has in another. After the first shock, she prophesied proudly, within her own mind, how soon his noble spirit would recover itself. Perhaps she anticipated other scenes in that undeveloped future, which might touch her own heart with a stronger thrill than even the marvellous change which was now working; perhaps the faint dawn of colour on her pale cheek came from an imagination far more immediate and personal than any dream which ever before had flushed the maiden firmament of Agnes Atheling's meditations. However that might be, she said not a single word upon the subject: she assumed to herself quietly the post of universal ministration, attended to the household wants as much as the little party, all excited and sublimed out of any recollection of ordinary necessities, would permit her; and lacking nothing in sympathy, yet quieter than any one else, insensibly to herself, formed the link between this little agitated world of private history and the larger world, not at all moved from its everyday balance, which lay calm and great without.

"I sign a universal amnesty," said Miss Anastasia abruptly, after a long silence—"himself, if he would consult his own interest, I could pass over *his* faults to-day."

"Poor Mr Reginald!" said Mrs Atheling, wiping her eyes. "I beg your pardon, Miss Rivers; he has done a great deal of wrong, but I am very sorry for him: I was so when he lost his son; ah, no doubt he thinks this is a very small matter after *that*."

"Hush, child, the man is *guilty*," said Miss Anastasia, with strong emphasis. "Young George Rivers went to his grave in peace. Whom the gods love die young; it was very well. I forgive his father if he withdraws; he will, if he has a spark of honour. The only person whom I am grieved for is Lionel—he, indeed, might have cause to complain. Agnes Atheling, do you know where he has gone?"

"No." Agnes affected no surprise that the question should be asked her, and did not even show any emotion. Marian, with a sudden impulse of generosity, got up instantly, and came to her sister. "Oh, Agnes, I am very sorry," said the little beauty, with her palpitating heart; and Marian put her pretty arms round Agnes's neck to console and comfort her, as Agnes might have done to Marian had Louis been in distress instead of joy.

Agnes drew herself instinctively out of her sister's embrace. She had no right to be looked upon as the representative of Lionel, yet she could not help speaking, in her confidence and pride in him, with a kindling cheek and rising heart. "I am not sorry for Mr Rivers *now*," said Agnes, firmly; "I was so while this secret was kept from him—while he was deceived; but I think no one who does him due credit can venture to pity him *now*."

Miss Anastasia roused herself a little at sound of the voice. This pride, which sounded a little like defiance, stirred the old lady's heart like the sound of a trumpet; she had more pleasure in it than she had felt in anything, save her first welcome of Louis a few hours ago. She looked steadily into the eyes of Agnes, who met her gaze without shrinking, though with a rapid variation of colour. Whatever imputations she herself might be subject to in consequence, Agnes could not sit by silent, and hear *him* either pitied or belied.

"I wonder, may I go and see Miss Rivers? would it be proper?" asked Rachel timidly, making a sudden diversion, as she had rather a habit of doing; "she wanted me to stay with her once; she was very kind to me."

"I suppose we must not call you the Honourable Rachel Rivers just yet—eh, little girl?" said Miss Anastasia, turning upon her; "and you, Marian, you little beauty, how shall you like to be Lady Winterbourne?"

"Lady Winterbourne! I always said she was to be for Louis," cried Rachel—"always—the first time I saw her; you know I did, Agnes; and often I wondered why she should be so pretty—she who did not want it, who was happy enough to have been ugly, if she had liked; but I see it now—I see the reason now!"

"Don't hide your head, little one; it is quite true," said Miss Anastasia, once more a little touched at her heart to see the beautiful little figure, fain to glide out of everybody's sight, stealing away in a moment into the natural refuge, the mother's shadow; while the mother, smiling and sobbing, had entirely given up all attempt at any show of self-command. "Agnes has something else to do in this hard-fighting world. You are the flower that must know neither winds nor storms. I don't speak to make you vain, you beautiful child. God gave you your lovely looks, as well as your strange fortune; and Agnes, child, lift up your head! the contest and the trial are for you; but not, God forbid it! as they came to *me*."

CHAPTER XXIX
THE RIVAL HEIRS

Louis and Rachel returned that night with Miss Anastasia to the Priory, which, the old lady said proudly—the family jointure house for four or five generations—should be their home till the young heir took possession of his paternal house. The time which followed was too busy, rapid, and exciting for a slow and detailed history. The first legal steps were taken instantly in the case, and proper notices served upon Lord Winterbourne. In Miss Anastasia's animated and anxious house dwelt the Tyrolese, painfully acquiring some scant morsels of English, very well contented with her present quarters, and only anxious to secure some extravagant preferment for her son. Mrs Atheling and her daughters had returned home, and Louis came and went constantly to town, actively engaged himself in all the arrangements, full of anxious plans and undertakings for the ease and benefit of the other parties concerned. Miss Anastasia, with a little reluctance, had given her consent to the young man's plan of a compromise, by which his uncle, unattacked and undisgraced, might retire from his usurped possessions with a sufficient and suitable income. The ideas of Louis were magnificent and princely. He would have been content to mulct himself of half the revenues of his inheritance, and scarcely would listen to the prudent cautions of his advisers. He was even reluctant that the first formal steps should be taken, before Mr Foggo and an eminent and well-known solicitor, personally acquainted with his uncle, had waited upon Lord Winterbourne. He was overruled; but this solemn deputation lost no time in proceeding on its mission. Speedy as they were, however, they were too late for the alarmed and startled peer. He had left home, they ascertained, very shortly after the late trial—had gone abroad, as it was supposed, leaving no information as to the time of his return. The only thing which could be done in the circumstances was hastened by the eager exertions of Louis. The two lawyers wrote a formal letter to Lord Winterbourne, stating their case, and making their offer, and despatched it to the Hall, to be forwarded to him.

No answer came, though Louis persuaded his agents to wait for it, and even to delay the legal proceedings. The only notice taken of it was a paragraph in one of the fashionable newspapers, to the effect that the late proceedings at Oxford, impugning the title of a respected nobleman, proved now to be a mere trick of some pettifogging lawyer, entirely unsupported, and likely to call forth proceedings for libel, involving a good deal of romantic family history, and extremely interesting to the public. After this, Louis could no longer restrain the natural progress of the matter. He gave it up, indeed, at once, and did not try; and Miss Anastasia pronounced emphatically one of her antique proverbs, "Whom the gods would destroy, they first make mad."

This was not the only business on the hands of Louis. He had found it impossible, on repeated trials, to see the Rector. At the Old Wood House it was said that Mr Rivers was from home; at his London lodgings he had not been heard of. The suit was given against him in the Ecclesiastical Courts, and Mr Mead, alone in the discharge of his duty, mourned over a stripped altar and desolated sanctuary, where the tall candles blazed no longer in the religious gloom. When it became evident at last that the Rector did not mean to give his young relative the interview he sought, Louis, strangely transformed as he was, from the petulant youth always ready to take offence, to the long-suffering man, addressed Lionel as his solicitors had addressed his uncle. He wrote a long letter, generous and full of hearty feeling; he reminded his kinsman of the favours he had himself accepted at his hands. He drew a very vivid picture of his own past and present position. He declared, with all a young man's fervour, that he could have no pleasure even in his own extraordinary change of fortune, were it the means of inflicting a vast and unmitigated loss upon his cousin. He threw himself upon Lionel's generosity—he appealed to his natural sense of justice—he used a hundred arguments which were perfectly suitable and in character from him, but which, certainly, no man as proud and as generous as himself could be expected to listen to; and, finally, ended with protesting an unquestionable claim upon Lionel—the claim of a man deeply indebted to, and befriended by him. The letter overflowed with the earnestness and sincerity of the writer; he assumed his case throughout with the most entire honesty, having no doubt whatever upon the subject, and confided his intentions and prospects to Lionel with a complete and anxious confidence, which he had not bestowed upon any other living man.

This letter called forth an answer, written from a country town in a remote part of England. The Rector wrote with an evident effort at cordiality. He declined all Louis's overtures in the most uncompromising terms, but congratulated him upon his altered circumstances. He said he had taken care to examine into the case before leaving London, and was thoroughly convinced of the justice of the new claim. "One thing I will ask of you," said Mr Rivers; "I only wait to resign my living until I can be sure of the next presentation falling into your hands: give it to Mr Mead. The cause of my withdrawal is entirely private and personal. I had resolved upon it months ago, and it has no connection whatever with recent circumstances. I hope no one thinks so meanly of me as to suppose I am dismayed by the substitution of another heir in my room. One thing in this matter has really wounded me, and that is the fact that no one concerned thought me worthy to know a secret so important, and one which it was alike my duty and my right to help to a satisfactory conclusion. I have lost nothing actual, so far as rank or means is concerned; but, more intolerable than any vulgar loss, I find a sudden cloud thrown upon the perfect sincerity and truth of some whom I have been disposed to trust as men trust Heaven."

The letter concluded with good wishes—that was all; there was no response to the confidence, no answer to the effusion of heartfelt and fervent feeling which had been in Louis's letter. The young man was not accustomed to be repulsed; perhaps, in all his life, it was the first time he had asked a favour from any one, and had Louis been poor and without friends, as he was or thought himself six months ago, such a tone would have galled him beyond endurance. But there is a charm in a gracious and relenting fortune. Louis, who had once been the very armadillo of youthful haughtiness, suddenly distinguished himself by the most magnanimous patience, would not take offence, and put away his kinsman's haughty letter, with regret, but without any resentment. Nothing was before him now but the plain course of events, and to them he committed himself frankly, resolved to do what could be done, but addressing no more appeals to the losing side.

Part of the Rector's letter Louis showed to Marian, and Marian repeated it to Agnes. It was cruel—it was unjust of Lionel—and he knew himself that it was. Agnes, it was possible, did not know—at all events, she had no right to betray to him the secrets of another; more than that, he knew the meaning now of the little book which he carried everywhere with him, and felt in his heart that *he* was the real person addressed. He knew all that quite as well as she did, as she tried, with a quivering lip and a proud wet eye, to fortify herself against the injustice of his reproach, but that did not hinder him from saying it. He was in that condition—known, perhaps, occasionally to most of us—when one feels a certain perverse pleasure in wounding one's dearest. He had no chance of mentioning her, who occupied so much of his thoughts, in any other way, and he would rather put a reproach upon Agnes than leave her alone altogether; perhaps she herself even, after all, at the bottom of her heart, was better satisfied to be referred to thus, than to be left out of his thoughts. They had never spoken to each other a single word which could be called wooing—now they were perhaps separated for ever—yet how strange a link of union, concord, and opposition, was between these two!

CHAPTER XXX
AN ADVENTURE

It was September—the time when all Englishmen of a certain "rank in life" burn with unconquerable longings to get as far away from home as possible—and there was nothing remarkable in the appearance of this solitary traveller pacing along Calais pier—nothing remarkable, except his own personal appearance, which was of a kind not easily overlooked. There was nothing to be read in his embrowned but refined face, nor in his high thoughtful forehead. It was a face of thought, of speculation, of a great and vigorous intellectual activity; but the haughty eyes looked at no one—the lips never moved even to address a child—there was no response to any passing glance of interest or inquiry. His head was turned towards England, over the long sinuous weltering waves of that stormy Channel which to-day pretended to be calm; but if he saw anything, it was something which appeared only in his own imagination—it was neither the far-away gleam, like a floating mist, of the white cliffs, nor the sunbeam coming down out of the heart of a cloud into the dark mid-current of that treacherous sea.

He had no plan of travel—no settled intentions indeed of any kind—but had been roaming about these three months in the restlessness of suspense, waiting for definite intelligence before he decided on his further course. An often-recurring fancy of returning home for a time had brought him to-day to this common highway of all nations from a secluded village among the Pyrenees; but he had not made up his mind to go home—he only lingered within sight of it, chafing his own disturbed spirit, and ready to be swayed by any momentary impulse. Though he had been disturbed for a time out of his study of the deepest secrets of human life, his mind was too eager not to have returned to it. He had come to feel that it would be sacrilege to proclaim again his own labouring and disordered thoughts in a place where he was set to speak of One, the very imagination of whom, if it was an imagination, was so immeasurably exalted above his highest elevation. A strange poetic justice had come upon Lionel Rivers—prosecuted for his extreme views at the time when he ceased to make any show of holding them—separating himself from his profession, and from the very name of a believer, at the moment when it began to dawn upon him that he believed—

and thrust asunder with a violent wrench and convulsion from the first and sole human creature who had come into his heart, at the very hour in which he discovered that his heart was no longer in his own power. He saw it all, the strange story of contradictory and perverse chances, and knew himself the greatest and strangest contradiction of the whole.

He gave no attention whatever to what passed round him, yet he heard the foreign voices—the English voices—for there was no lack of his countrymen. It was growing dark rapidly, and the shadowy evening lights and mists were stealing far away to sea. He turned to go back to his hotel, turning his face away from his own country, when at the moment a voice fell upon his ear, speaking his own tongue: "You will abet an impostor—you who know nothing of English law, and are already a marked man." These were the words spoken in a very low, clear, hissing tone, which Lionel heard distinctly only because it was well known to him. The speaker was wrapt in a great cloak, with a travelling-cap over his eyes; and the person he addressed was a little vivacious Italian, with a long olive face, smooth-shaven cheeks, and sparkling lively eyes, who seemed much disconcerted and doubtful what to do. The expression of Lionel's face changed in an instant—he woke out of his moody dream to alert and determined action; he drew back a step to let them pass, and then followed. The discussion was animated and eager between them, sometimes in English, sometimes in Italian, apparently as caprice guided the one or the other. Lionel did not listen to what they said, but he followed them home.

The old Italian parted with his companion at the door of the hotel where Lionel himself was lodged; there the Englishman in the cloak and cap lingered to make an appointment. "At eleven to-morrow," said again that sharp hissing voice. Lionel stepped aside into the shadow as the stranger turned reluctantly away; he did not care for making further investigations to ascertain *his* identity—it was Lord Winterbourne.

He took the necessary steps immediately. It was easy to find out where the Italian was, in a little room at the top of the house, the key of which he paused to take down before he went up-stairs. Lionel waited again till the old man had made his way to his lofty lodging. He was very well acquainted with all the details of Louis's case; he had, in fact, seen Charlie Atheling a few days before he left London, and satisfied himself of the nature of his young kinsman's claim—it was too important to himself to be forgotten. He remembered perfectly the Italian doctor Serrano who had been present, and could testify to the marriage of the late Lord Winterbourne. Lionel scaled the great staircase half-a-dozen steps at a time, and reached the door immediately after the old man had entered, and before he had struck his light. The Rector knocked softly. With visible perturbation, and in a sharp tone of self-defence, the Italian called out in a very good French to know who was there. Dr Serrano was a patriot and a plotter, and used to domiciliary visitations. Lionel answered him in English, asked if he were Doctor Serrano, and announced himself as a friend of Charles Atheling. Then the door opened slowly, and with some jealousy. Lionel passed into the room without waiting for an invitation. "You are going to England on a matter of the greatest importance," said the Rector, with excitement—"to restore the son of your friend to his inheritance; yet I find you, with the serpent at your ear, listening to Lord Winterbourne."

The Italian started back in amaze. "Are you the devil?" said Doctor Serrano, with a comical perturbation.

"No; instead of that, you have just left him," said Lionel; "but I am a friend, and know all. This man persuades you not to go on—by accident I caught the sound of his voice saying so. He has the most direct personal interest in the case; it is ruin and disgrace to him. Your testimony may be of the greatest importance—why do you linger? why do you listen to him?"

"Really, you are hot-headed; it is so with youth," said Doctor Serrano, "when we will move heaven and earth for one friend. He tells me the child is dead—that this is another. I know not—it may be true."

"It is not true," said Lionel. "I will tell you who I am—the next heir if Lord Winterbourne is the true holder of the title—there is my card. I have the strongest interest in resisting this claim if I did not know it to be true. It can be proved that this is the same boy who was brought from Italy an infant. I can prove it myself; it is known to a whole village. If you choose it, confront me with Lord Winterbourne."

"No; I believe you—you are a gentleman," said Doctor Serrano, turning over the card in his hand—and the old man added with enthusiasm, "and a hero for a friend!"

"You believe me?" said Lionel, who could not restrain the painful smile which crossed his face at the idea of his heroism in the cause of Louis. "Will you stay, then, another hour within reach of Lord Winterbourne?"

The Italian shrugged his shoulders. "I will break with him; he is ever false," said the old man. "What besides can I do?"

"I will tell you," said Lionel. "The boat sails in an hour—come with me at once, let me see you safe in England. I shall attend to your comfort with all my power. There is time for a good English bed at Dover, and an undisturbed rest. Doctor Serrano, for the sake of the oppressed, and because you are a philosopher, and understand the weakness of human nature, will you come with me?"

The Italian glanced lovingly at the couch which invited him—at the slippers and the pipe which waited to make him comfortable—then he glanced up at the dark and resolute countenance of Lionel, who, high in his chivalric honour, was determined rather to sleep at Serrano's door all night than to let him out of his hands. "Excellent young man! you are not a philosopher!" said the rueful Doctor; but he had a quick eye, and was accustomed to judge men. "I will go with you," he added seriously, "and some time, for liberty and Italy, you will do as much for me."

It was a bargain, concluded on the spot. An hour after, almost within sight of Lord Winterbourne, who was pacing the gloomy pier by night in his own gloom of guilty thought, the old man and the young man embarked for England. A few hours later the little Italian slept under an English roof, and the young Englishman looked up at the dizzy cliff, and down at the foaming sea, too much excited to think of rest. The next morning Lionel carried off his prize to London, and left him in the hands of Charlie Atheling. Then, seeing no one, speaking to no one, without lingering an hour in his native country, he turned back and went away. He had made up his mind now to remain at Calais till the matter was entirely decided—then to resign his benefice—and then, with *things* and not *thoughts* around him in the actual press and contact of common life, to read, if he could, the grand secret of a true existence, and decide his fate.

CHAPTER XXXI
THE TRIAL

Lord Winterbourne had been in Italy, going over the ground which Charlie Atheling had already examined so carefully. Miss Anastasia's proverb was coming true. He who all his life had been so wary, began to calculate madly, with an insane disregard of all the damning facts against him, on overturning, by one bold stroke, the careful fabric of the young lawyer. He sought out and found the courier Monte, whom he himself had established in his little mountain-inn. Monte was a faithful servant enough to his employer of the time, but he was not scrupulous, and had no great conscience. He undertook, without much objection, for the hire which Lord Winterbourne gave him, to say anything Lord Winterbourne pleased. He had been present at the marriage; and if the old Doctor could have been delayed, or turned back, or even kidnapped—which was in the foiled plotter's scheme, if nothing better would serve—Monte, being the sole witness of the ceremony present, might have made it out a mock marriage, or at least delayed the case, and thrown discredit upon the union. It was enough to show what mad shifts even a wise intriguer might be driven to trust in. He believed it actually possible that judge and jury would ignore all the other testimony, and trust to the unsupported word of his lying witness. He did not pause to think, tampering with truth as he had been all his life, and trusting no man, what an extreme amount of credulity he expected for himself.

But even when Doctor Serrano escaped him—when the trial drew nearer day by day—when Louis's agents came in person, respectful and urgent, to make their statement to him—and when he became aware that his case was naught, and that he had no evidence whatever to depend on save that of Monte, his wild confidence did not yield. He refused with disdain every offer of a compromise; he commanded out of his presence the bearers of that message of forbearance and forgiveness; he looked forward with a blind defiance of his fate miserable to see. He gave orders that preparations should be made at Winterbourne for the celebration of his approaching triumph. That autumn he had invited to his house a larger party than usual; and though few came, and those the least reputable, there was no want of sportsmen in the covers, nor merry-makers at the Hall: he himself was restless, and did not continue there, even for the sake of his guests, but made incessant journeys to London, and kept in constant personal attendance on himself the courier Monte. He was the object of incessant observation, and the gossip of half the county: he had many enemies; and many of those who were disposed to take his part, had heard and been convinced by the story of Louis. Almost every one, indeed, who did hear of it, and remembered the boy in his neglected but noble youth, felt the strange probability and *vraisemblance* of the tale; and as the time drew nearer, the interest grew. It was known that the new claimant of the title lived in Miss Anastasia's house, and that she was the warmest supporter of his claim. The people of Banburyshire were proud of Miss Anastasia; but she was Lord Winterbourne's enemy. Why? That old tragedy began to be spoken of once more in whispers; other tales crept into circulation; he was a bad man; everybody knew something of him—enough ground to judge him on; and if he was capable of all these, was he not capable of this?

As the public voice grew thus, like the voice of doom, the doomed man went on in his reckless and unreasoning confidence; the warnings of his opponents and of his friends seemed to be alike fruitless. No extent of self-delusion could have justified him at any time in thinking himself popular, yet he seemed to have a certain insane conviction now, that he had but to show himself in the court to produce an immediate reaction in his favour. He even said so, shaken out of all his old self-restrained habits, boasting with a vain braggadocio to his guests at the Hall; and people began, with a new impulse of pity, to wonder if his reason was touched, and to hint vaguely to each other that the shock had unsettled his mind.

The trial came on at the next assize; it was long, elaborate, and painful. On the very eve of this momentous day, Louis himself had addressed an appeal to his uncle, begging him, at the last moment when he could withdraw with honour, to accept the compromise so often and so anxiously proposed to him. Lord Winterbourne tore the letter in two, and put it in his pocket-book. "I shall use it," he said to the messenger, "when this business is over, to light the bonfire on Badgeley Hill."

The trial came on accordingly, without favour or private arrangement—a fair struggle of force against force. The evidence on the side of the prosecutor was laid down clearly, particular by particular; the marriage of the late Lord Winterbourne to the young Italian—the entry in his pocket-book, sworn to by Miss Anastasia—the birth of the children—their journey from Italy to London, from London to Winterbourne—and the identity of the boy Louis with the present claimant of the title—clearly, calmly, deliberately, everything was proved. It took two days to go over the evidence; then came the defence. Without an overwhelming array of witnesses on the other side—without proving perjury on the part of these—what could Lord Winterbourne answer to such a charge as this?

He commenced, through his lawyer, by a vain attempt to brand Louis over again with illegitimacy, to sully the name of his dead brother, and represent him a villanous deceiver. It was allowed, without controversy, that Louis was the son of the old lord; and then Monte was placed in the witness-box to prove that the marriage was a mock marriage, so skilfully performed as to cheat herself, her family, the old quick-witted Serrano, whose testimony had pleased every one—all the people present, in short, except his own acute and philosophical self.

The fellow was bold, clever, and scrupulous, but he was not prepared for such an ordeal. His attention distracted by the furious contradictory gestures of Doctor Serrano, whose cane could scarcely be kept out of action— by the stern, steady glance of Miss Anastasia, whom he recognised—he was no match for the skilful cross-examiners who had him in hand. He hesitated, prevaricated, altered his testimony. He held, with a grim obstinacy, to unimportant trifles, and made admissions at the same moment which struck at the very root of his own credibility as a witness. He was finally ordered to sit down by the voice of the judge himself, which rung in the fellow's ears like thunder. That was all the case for the defence! Even Lord Winterbourne's counsel coloured for shame as he made the miserable admission. The jury scarcely left the court; there was no doubt remaining on the mind of the audience. The verdict was pronounced solemnly, like a passionless voice of justice, as it was, for the plaintiff. There was no applause—no exultation—a universal human horror and disgust at the strange depravity they had just witnessed, put down every demonstration of feeling. People drew away from the neighbourhood of Lord Winterbourne as from a man in a pestilence. He left the court almost immediately, with his hat over his eyes—his witness following as he best could; then came a sudden revulsion of feeling. The best men in the county hurried towards Louis, who sat, pale and excited, by the side of his elder and his younger sister. Congratulatory good wishes poured upon him on every side. As they left the court slowly, a guard of honour surrounded this heir and hero of romance; and as he emerged into the street the air rang with a cheer for the new Lord Winterbourne. They called him "My lord," as he stood on the step of Miss Anastasia's carriage, which she herself entered as if it had been a car of triumph. *She* called him "My lord," making a proud obeisance to him, as a mother might have done to her son, a new-made king; and they drove off slowly, with riders in their train, amid the eager observation of all the passengers—the new Lord Winterbourne!

The old one hastened home on foot, no one observing him—followed far off, like a shadow, by his attendant villain—unobserved, and almost unheeded, entered the Hall; thrust with his own hand some necessaries into his travelling-bag, gathered his cloak around him, and was gone. Winterbourne Hall that night was left in the custody of the strangers who had been his guests, an uneasy and troubled company, all occupied with projects of departure to-morrow. Once more the broad chill moonlight fell on the noble park, as when Louis and his sister, desolate and friendless, passed out from its lordly gates into midnight and the vacant world. Scarcely a year! but what a change upon all the actors and all the passions of that moonlight October night!

CHAPTER XXXII
ESPOUSALS

It was winter, but the heavens were bright—a halcyon day among the December glooms. All the winds lay still among the withered ferns, making a sighing chorus in the underground of Badgeley Wood; but the white clouds, thinner than the clouds of summer, lay becalmed upon the chill blue sky, and the sun shone warm under the hedgerows, and deluded birds were perching out upon the hawthorn bows; the green grass brightened under the morning light; the wan waters shone; the trees which had no leaves clustered their branches together, with a certain pathos in their nakedness, and made a trellised shadow here and there over the wintry stream; and, noble as in the broadest summer, in the sheen of the December sunshine lay Oxford, jewelled like a bride, gleaming out upon the tower of Maudlin, flashing abroad into the firmament from fair St Mary, twinkling with innumerable gem-points from all the lesser cupolas and spires. In the midst of all, this sunshine retreated in pure defeat and failure, from that sombre old heathen, with his heavy dome—but only brightened all the more upon those responsive and human inhabitants dwelling there from the olden ages, and native to the soil. There was a fresh breath from the broad country, a hum of life in the air, a twitter of hardy birds among the trees. It was one of those days which belong to no season, but come, like single blessings, one by one, throwing a gleam across the darker half of the year. Though it was in December instead of May, it was as fair "a bridal of the earth and sky" as poet could have wished to see; but the season yielded no flowers to strew upon the grassy footpath between the Old Wood Lodge and the little church of Winterbourne; they did not need them who trod that road to-day.

Hush, they are coming home—seeing nothing but an indefinite splendour in the earth and in the sky—sweet in the dews of their youth— touched to the heart—to that very depth and centre where lie all ecstasies and tears. Walking together arm in arm, in their young humility—scarcely aware of the bridal train behind them—in an enchantment of their own; now coming back to that old little room, with its pensive old memories of hermit life and solitude—this quiet old place, which never before was lighted up with such a gleam of splendid fortune and happy hope.

You would say it was Marian Atheling, "with the smile on her lip, and the tear in her eye" —the very same lovely vision whom the lad Louis saw some eighteen months ago at the garden gate. But you would be mistaken; for it is not Marian—it is the young Lady Winterbourne. This one is quite as beautiful for a consolation—almost more so in her bridal blush, and sunshine, and tears—and for a whole hour by the village clock has been a peeress of the realm.

This is what it has come to, after all—what they must all come to, those innocent young people—even Rachel, who is as wild as a child, in her first genuine and unalarmed outburst of youthful jubilation—even Agnes, who through all this joy carries a certain thoughtful remembrance in her dark eyes—possibly even Charlie, who fears no man, but is a little shy of every womankind younger than Miss Anastasia. There are only one or two strangers; but the party almost overflows Miss Bridget's parlour, where the old walls smile with flowers, and the old apartment, like an ancient handmaid, receives them with a prim and antique grace—a little doubtful, yet half hysterical with joy.

But it does not last very long, this crowning festival. By-and-by the hero and the heroine go away; then the guests one by one; then the family, a little languid, a little moved with the first inroad among them, disperse to their own apartments, or to a meditative ramble out of doors; and when the twilight falls, you could almost suppose Miss Bridget, musing too over the story of another generation, sitting before the fire in her great old chair, with no companion but the flowers.

This new event seemed somehow to consolidate and make certain that wonderful fortune of Louis, which until then had looked almost too much like a romance to be realised. His uncle had made various efforts to question and set aside the verdict which transferred to the true heir his name and inheritance—efforts in which even the lawyers whom he had employed at the trial, and who were not over-scrupulous, had refused any share. The attempt was entirely fruitless—an insane resistance to the law, which was irresistible; and the Honourable Reginald Rivers, whom some old sycophants who came in his way still flattered with his old title, was now at Baden, a great man enough in his own circle, rich in the allowance from his nephew, which he was no longer too proud to accept. He alone of all men expressed any disapprobation of Louis's marriage—he whose high sense of family honour revolted from the idea of a *mesalliance*—and one other individual, who had something of a more reasonable argument. We hasten to extract, according to a former promise, the following pathetic paragraph from the pages of the *Mississippi Gazette*:—

"I have just heard of the marriage of the young Lord W—— with the beautiful M—— A——. Well!—is that so wonderful? Oh, visionary dream! That thou shouldst pause to comment upon a common British bargain—the most ordinary arrangement of this conventional and rotten life? What is a heart in comparison with a title?—true love in the balance of a coronet? Oh, my country, *thou* hast not come to this! But for these mercenary and heartless parents—but for the young mind dazzled with the splendid cheat of rank—oh heaven, what true felicity—what poetic rapture—what a home thou mightst have seen! For she was beautiful as the day when it breaks upon the rivers and the mountains of my native land! It is enough—a poet's fate would have been all incomplete without this fiery trial. Farewell, M——! Farewell, lovely deluded victim of a false society! Some time out of your hollow splendour you will think of a true heart and weep!"

CHAPTER XXXIII
AN OLD FRIEND

"The Winterbournes" had been for some time at home—they were now in London, and Marian had appeared at court in the full splendour of that young beauty of hers; which never had dazzled any one at home as it dazzled every one now. She and her handsome young husband were the lions of the season, eagerly sought after in "the best society." Their story had got abroad, as stories which are at all remarkable have such a wonderful faculty of getting; and strangers whom Marian had never seen before, were delighted to make her acquaintance—charmed to know her sister, who had so much genius, and wrote such delightful books, and, most extraordinary of all, extremely curious and interested about Charlie, the wonderful young brother who had found out the mystery. At one of the fashionable assemblies, where Louis and Marian, Rachel and Agnes, were pointed out eagerly on all sides, and commented upon as "such fresh unsophisticated young creatures—such a group! so picturesque, so interesting!" they became aware, all of them, with different degrees of embarrassment and pain, that Mrs Edgerley was in the company. Louis found her out last of all. She could not possibly fail to notice them; and the young man, anxious to save her pain, made up his mind at once to be the first to address her. He went forward gravely, with more than usual deference in his manner. She recognised him in a moment, started with a little surprise and a momentary shock, but immediately rushed forward with her most charming air of enthusiasm, caught his hand, and overwhelmed him with congratulations. "Oh, I should be so shocked if you supposed that I entertained any prejudice because of poor dear papa!" cried Mrs Edgerley. "Of course he meant no harm; of course he did not know any better. I am so charmed to see you! I am sure we shall make most capital cousins and firm allies. Positively you look quite grave at me. Oh, I assure you, family feuds are entirely out of fashion, and no one ever quarrels with *me*! I am dying to see those sweet girls!"

And very much amazed, and filled with great perturbation, those sweet girls were, when Mrs Edgerley came up to them, leaning upon Louis's arm, bestowed upon them all a shower of those light perfumy kisses which

Marian and Agnes remembered so well, and, declaring Lady Winterbourne far too young for a chaperone, took her place among them. Amazed as they were at this sudden renewal of old friendship, none of them desired to resist it; and before they were well aware, they found themselves engaged, the whole party, to Mrs Edgerley's next "reception," when "every one would be so charmed to see them!" "Positively, my love, you are looking quite lovely," whispered the fine lady into the shrinking ear of Marian. "I always said so. I constantly told every one you were the most perfect little beauty in the world; and then that charming book of Miss Atheling's, which every one was wild about! and your brother—now, do you know, I wish so very much to know your brother. Oh, I am sure you could persuade him to come to my Thursday. Tell him every one comes; no one ever refuses *me*! I shall send him a card to-morrow. Now, may I leave my cause in your hands?"

"We will try," said Marian, who, though she bore her new dignities with extraordinary self-possession on the whole, was undeniably shy of Agnes's first fashionable patroness. The invitation was taken up as very good fun indeed, by all the others. They resolved to make a general assault upon Charlie, and went home in great glee with their undertaking. Nor was Charlie, after all, so hard to be moved as they expected. He twisted the pretty note in his big fingers with somewhat grim amusement, and said he did not mind. With this result Mrs Atheling showed the greatest delight, for the good mother began to speculate upon a wife for Charlie, and to be rather afraid of some humble beauty catching her boy's eye before he had "seen the world."

With almost the feeling of people in a dream, Agnes and Marian entered once more those well-remembered rooms of Mrs Edgerley, in which they had gained their first glimpse of the world; and Charlie, less demonstrative of his feelings, but not without a remembrance of the past, entered these same portals where he had exchanged that first glance of instinctive enmity with the former Lord Winterbourne. The change was almost too extraordinary to be realised even by the persons principally concerned. Marian, who had been but Agnes Atheling's pretty and shy sister, came in now first of the party, the wife of the head of her former patroness's family. Agnes, a diffident young genius then, full of visionary ideas of fame, had now her own known and acknowledged place, but had gone far beyond it, in the heart which did not palpitate any longer with the glorious young fancies of a visionary ambition; and Charlie, last of all—Charlie, who had tumbled out of the Islington fly to take charge of his sisters—a big boy, clumsy and manful, whom Lord Winterbourne smiled at, as he passed, with his ungenial smile—Charlie, almost single-handed, had thrust the usurper from his seat, and placed the true heir in his room. No wonder that the Athelings were somewhat dizzy with recollections when they came among all the fashionable people who were charmed to see them, and found their way at last to the boudoir where Agnes and Marian had looked at the faces and the diamonds, on that old Thursday of Mrs Edgerley's, which sparkled still in their recollection, the beginning of their fate.

But though Louis and Marian, and Agnes and Rachel, were all extremely attractive, had more or less share in the romance, and were all more or less handsome, Charlie was without dispute the lion of the night. Mrs Edgerley fluttered about with him, holding his great arm with her pretty hand, and introducing him to every one; and with a smile, rueful, comical, half embarrassed, half ludicrous, Charlie, who continued to be very shy of ladies, suffered himself to be dragged about by the fashionable enchantress. He had very little to say—he was such a big fellow, so unmanageable in a delicate crowd of fine ladies, with draperies like gossamer, and, to do him justice, very much afraid of the dangerous steering; but Charlie's "manners," though they would have overwhelmed with distress his anxious mother, rather added to his "success." "It was he who conducted the whole case." "I do not wonder! Look, what a noble head! What a self-absorbed expression! What a power of concentration!" were the sweet and audible whispers which rang around him; and the more sensible observers of the scene, who saw the secret humour in Charlie's upper-lip, slightly curved with amusement, acute, but not unkindly, and caught now and then a gleam of his keen eye, which, when it met with a response, always made a momentary brightening of the smile—were disposed to give him full credit for all the power imputed to him. Mrs Edgerley was in the highest delight—he was a perfect success for a lion. Lions, as this patroness of the fine arts knew by experience, were sadly apt to betray themselves, to be thrown off their balance, to talk nonsense. But Charlie, who was not given to talking, who was still so delightfully clumsy, and made such a wonderful bow, was perfectly charming; Mrs Edgerley declared she was quite in love with him. After all, natural feeling put out of the question, she had no extraordinary occasion to identify herself with the resentments or enmities of that ruined plotter at Baden; and he must have been a worthy father, indeed, who had moved Mrs Edgerley to shut her heart or her house to the handsome young couple, whom everybody delighted to honour, or to the hero of a fashionable romance, which was spoken of everywhere. She had no thought of any such sacrifice; she established the most friendly relations instantly with her charming young cousins. She extended the kindly title, with the most fascinating amiability, to Agnes and Charlie. She overwhelmed the young lawyer with compliments and invitations. He had a much stronger hold upon her fickle fancy than the author of *Hope Hazlewood*. Mrs Edgerley was delighted to speak to all her acquaintances of Mr Atheling, "who conducted all the case against poor dear papa—did everything himself, I assure you—and such a charming modesty of genius, such a wonderful force and character! Oh, any one may be jealous who pleases; I cannot help it. I quite adore that clever young man."

Charlie took it all very quietly; he concerned himself as little about the adoration of Mrs Edgerley, as he did about the secret scrutiny of his mother concerning every young woman who chanced to cross the path of her son. Young women were the only created things whom Charlie was afraid of, and what his own secret thoughts might be upon this important question, nobody could tell.

CHAPTER XXXIV
SETTLING DOWN

Many lesser changes had been involved in the great revolution which made the nameless Louis head of the family, and conferred upon him the estates and title of Lord Winterbourne: scarcely any one, indeed, in the immediate circle of the two families of Rivers and Atheling, the great people and the small, remained uninfluenced by the change of sovereignty, except Miss Anastasia, whose heart and household charities were manifestly widened, but to whom no other change except the last, and grand one, was like to come. The Rector kept his word; as soon as he heard of the definite settlement of that great question of Louis's claim, he himself resigned his benefice; and one of the first acts of the new Lord Winterbourne was to answer the only request of Lionel, by conferring it upon Mr Mead. After that, Lionel made a settlement upon his sister of all the property which belonged to them, enough to make a modest maidenly income for the gentle invalid, and keep her in possession of all the little luxuries which seemed essential to her life. For himself, he retained a legacy of a thousand pounds which had been left to him several years before. This was the last that was known of the Rector—he disappeared into entire gloom and obscurity after he had made this final arrangement. It was sometimes possible to hear of him, for English travellers, journeying through unfamiliar routes, did not fail to note the wandering English gentleman who seemed to travel for something else than pleasure, and whose motives and objects no one knew; but where to look for him next, or what his occupations were, neither Louis nor his friends, in spite of all their anxious inquiries, could ever ascertain.

And Mr Mead was now the rector, and reigned in Lionel's stead. A new rectory, all gabled and pinnacled, more "correct" than the model it followed, and truer to its period than the truest original in Christendom, rose rapidly between the village and the Hall; and Mr Mead, whose altar had been made bare by the iconoclastic hands of authority, began to exhibit some little alteration in his opinions as he grew older, held modified views as to the priesthood, and cast an eye of visible kindness upon the Honourable Rachel Rivers. The sentiment, however, was not at all reciprocal; no one believed that Rachel was really as old as Louis—older than the pretty matron Marian, older even than Agnes. She had never been a girl until now—and Rachel cared a great deal more for the invalid Lucy in her noiseless shadowy chamber in the Old Wood House, than for all the rectors and all the curates in the world. *She* was fancy free, and promised to remain so; and Marian had already begun with a little horror to entertain the idea that Rachel possibly might never marry at all.

The parent Athelings themselves were not unmoved by the changes of their children. Charlie was to be received as a partner into the firm which Mr Foggo, by dint of habit, still clung to, as soon as he had attained his one-and-twentieth year. Agnes, as these quiet days went on, grew both in reputation and in riches, girl though she still was; and the youngest of them was Lady Winterbourne! All these great considerations somewhat dazzled the eyes of the confidential clerk of Messrs Cash, Ledger, & Co., as he turned over his books upon that desk where he had once placed Agnes's fifty-pound notes, the beginning of the family fortune. Bellevue came to be mightily out of the way when Louis and Marian were in town living in so different a quarter; and Mr Atheling wearied of the City, and Mamma concluded that the country air would be a great deal better for Bell and Beau. So Mr Atheling accepted a retiring allowance, the half of his previous income, from the employers whom he had served so long. The whole little household, even including Susan, removed to the country, where Marian had been delighting herself in the superintendence of the two or three additional rooms built to the Old Wood Lodge, which were so great a surprise to Mamma when she found them, risen as at the touch of a fairy's wand. The family settled there at once in unpretending comfort, taking farewell affectionately of Miss Willsie and Mr Foggo, but not forgetting Bellevue.

And here Agnes pursued her vocation, making very little demonstration of it, the main pillar for the mean time, and crowning glory of her father's house. Her own mind and imagination had been profoundly impressed, almost in spite of herself, by that last known act of Lionel's—his hasty journey to London with Doctor Serrano. It was the kind of act beyond all others to win upon a temperament so generous and sensitive, which a more ostentatious generosity might have disgusted and repelled; and perhaps the very uncertainty in which they remained concerning him kept up the lurking "interest" in Agnes Atheling's heart. It was possible that he might appear any day at their very doors; it was possible that he never might be seen again. It was not easy to avoid speculating upon him—what he was thinking, where he was?—and when, in that spontaneous delight of her young genius, which yet had suffered no diminution, Agnes's thoughts glided into impersonation, and fairy figures gathered round her, and one by one her fables grew, in the midst of the thread of story—in the midst of what people called, to the young author's amusement, "an elaborate development of character, the result of great study and observation"— thoughts came to her mind, and words to her lip, which she supposed no one could thoroughly understand save *one*. Almost unconsciously she shadowed his circumstances and his story in many a bright imagination of her own; and contrasted with the real one half-a-dozen imaginary Lionels, yet always ending in finding him the noblest type of action in that great crisis of his career. It blended somehow strangely with all that was most serious in her work; for when Agnes had to speak of faith, she spoke of it with the fervour with which one addresses an individual, opening her heart to show the One great Name enshrined in it to another, who, woe for him, in his wanderings so sadly friendless, knew not that Lord.

So the voice of the woman who dwelt at home went out over the world; it charmed multitudes who thought of nothing but the story it told, delighted some more who recognised that sweet faulty grace of youth, that generous young directness and simplicity which made the fable truth. If it ever reached to one who felt himself addressed in it, who knew the words, the allusions, that noble craft of genius, which, addressing all, had still a private voice for one—if there was such a man somewhere, in the desert or among the mountains far away, wandering where he seldom heard the tongue of his country, and never saw a face he recognised, Agnes never knew.

But after this fashion time went on with them all. Then there came a second heir, another Louis to the Hall at Winterbourne—and it was very hard to say whether this young gentleman's old aunt or his young aunt, the Honourable Rachel, or the Honourable Anastasia, was most completely out of her wits at this glorious epoch in the history of the House. Another event of the most startling and extraordinary description took place very shortly after the christening of Marian's miraculous baby. Charlie was one-and-twenty; he was admitted into the firm, and the young man, who was one of the most "rising young men" in his profession, took to himself a holiday, and went abroad without any one knowing much about it. No harm in that; but when Charlie returned, he brought with him a certain Signora Giulia, a very amazing companion indeed for this taciturn hero, who was afraid of young ladies. He took her down at once to Winterbourne, to present her to his mother and sisters. He had the grace to blush, but really was not half so much ashamed of himself as he ought to have been. For the pretty young Italian turned out to be cousin to Louis and Rachel—a delicate little beauty, extremely proud of the big young lover, who had carried her off from her mother's house six weeks ago: and we are grieved to acknowledge that Charlie henceforth showed no fear whatever, scarcely even the proper awe of a dutiful husband, in the presence of Mrs Charles Atheling.

CHAPTER XXXV
THE END

Agnes Atheling was alone in old Miss Bridget's parlour; it was a fervent day of July, and all the country lay in a hush and stillness of exceeding sunshine, which reduced all the common sounds of life, far and near, to a drowsy and languid hum—the midsummer's luxurious voice. The little house was perfectly still. Mrs Atheling was at the Hall, Papa in Oxford, and Hannah, whose sole beatific duty it was to take care of the children, and who envied no one in the world save the new nurse to the new baby, had taken out Bell and Beau. The door was open in the fearless fashion and license of the country. Perhaps Susan was dozing in the kitchen, or on the sunny outside bench by the kitchen door. There was not a sound about the house save the deep dreamy hum of the bees among the roses—those roses which clustered thick round the old porch and on the wall. Agnes sat by the open window, in a very familiar old occupation, making a frock for little Bell, who was six years old now, and appreciated pretty things. Agnes was not quite so young as she used to be—four years, with a great many events in them, had enlarged the maiden mind, which still was as fresh as a child's. She was changed otherwise: the ease which those only have who are used to the company of people of refinement, had added another charm to her natural grace. As she sat with her work on her knee, in her feminine attitude and occupation, making a meditative pause, bowing her head upon her hand, thinking of something, with those quiet walls of home around her— the open door, the open window, and no one else visible in the serene and peaceful house, she made, in her fair and thoughtful young womanhood, as sweet a type as one could desire of the serene and happy confidence of a quiet English home.

She did not observe any one passing; she was not thinking, perhaps, of any one hereabout who was like to pass—but she heard a step entering at the door. She scarcely looked up, thinking it some member of the family— scarcely moved even when the door of the parlour opened wider, and the step came in. Then she looked up—started up—let her work drop out of her hands, and, gazing with eagerness in the bronzed face of the stranger, uttered a wondering exclamation. He hastened to her, holding out his hand. "Mr Rivers?" cried Agnes, in extreme surprise and agitation—"is it *you*?"

What he said was some hasty faltering expressions of delight in seeing her, and they gazed at each other with their mutual "interest," glad, yet constrained. "We have tried often to find out where you were," said Agnes—"I mean Louis; he has been very anxious. Have you seen him? When did you come home?"

"I have seen no one save you."

"But Louis has been very anxious," said Agnes, with a little confusion. "We have all tried to discover where you were. Is it wrong to ask where you have been?"

But Lionel did not at all attend to her questions. He was less self-possessed than she was; he seemed to have only one idea at the present moment, so far as was visible, and that he simply expressed over again—"I am very glad—happy—to see you here and alone."

"Oh!" said Agnes with a nervous tremor—"I—I was asking, Mr Rivers, where you had been?"

This time he began to attend to her. "I have been everywhere," he said, "except where pleasure was. I have been on fields of battles—in places of wretchedness. I have come to tell you something—you only. Do you remember our conversation once by Badgeley Wood?"

"Yes."

"You gave me a talisman, Agnes," said the speaker, growing more excited; "I have carried it all over the world."

"Well," said Agnes as he paused. She looked at him very earnestly, without even a blush at the sound of her own name.

"Well—better than well!" cried Lionel; "wonderful—invincible—divine! I went to try your spell—I who trusted nothing—at the moment when everything had failed me—even you. I put yonder sublime Friend of yours to the experiment—I dared to do it! I took his name to the sorrowful, as you bade me. I cast out devils with his name, as the sorcerers tried to do. I put all the hope I could have in life upon the trial. Now I come to tell you the issue; it is fit that you should know."

Agnes leaned forward towards him, listening eagerly; she could not quite tell what she expected—a confession of faith.

"I am a man of ambition," said Lionel, turning in a moment from the high and solemn excitement of his former speech, with a sudden smile like a gleam of sunshine. "You remember my projects when I was heir of Winterbourne. You knew them, though I did not tell you; now I have found a cave in a wild mining district among a race of giants. I am Vicar of Botallach, among the Cornish men—have been for four-and-twenty hours—that is the end."

Agnes had put out her hand to him in the first impulse of joy and congratulation; a second thought, more subtle, made her pause, and blush, and draw back. Lionel was not so foolish as to wait the end of this self-controversy. He left his seat, came to her side, took the hand firmly into his own, which she half gave, and half withdrew—did not blush, but grew pale, with the quiet concern of a man who was about deciding the happiness of his life. "The end, but the beginning too," said Lionel, with a tremor in his voice. "Agnes hear me still—I have something more to say."

She did not answer a word; she lifted her eyes to his face with one hurried, agitated momentary glance. Something more! but the whole tale was in the look. *They* did not know very well what words followed, and neither do we.